Adventure
Activity

Part 1 • Spies   Part 3 • Pirates
Part 2 • Detectives   Part 4 • Explorers

zigzag

CONTENTS

Produced by Zigzag Publishing,
a division of Quadrillion Publishing Ltd.
Godalming Business Centre, Woolsack
Way, Godalming, Surrey GU7 1XW

Written by Hazel Songhurst
Devised by Robin Wright
Illustrated by Dave McTaggart, Kate
Buxton, Teresa Foster, Rachael O'Neill
Edited by Nicola Wright
Designed by Chris Leishman
Photographs by Tony Potter

This edition distributed in the U.S. by SMITHMARK PUBLISHERS
a division of U.S. Media Holdings, Inc. 16 East 32nd Street,
New York, NY 10016

Copyright © 1997 Zigzag Publishing Ltd

Colour separations by RCS Graphics Ltd, Leeds
Printed in Singapore

ISBN 0-7651-9324-8

ABOUT THIS BOOK

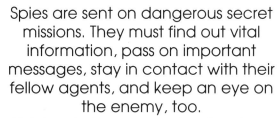

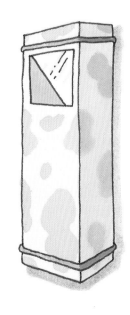

Spies are sent on dangerous secret missions. They must find out vital information, pass on important messages, stay in contact with their fellow agents, and keep an eye on the enemy, too.

This book shows you, step-by-step, how to play at being a spy and how to make the spy equipment for your mission. There are lots of ideas for disguises and a periscope to make so you can spy around corners and over walls!

Learn how to send your secret messages using special written codes and a Morse Code flasher, or make them disappear and then reappear with homemade invisible ink!

There are also plenty of tips on how to be a spy, with tricks and skills to practice. You will see how to set up your own spy-traps, take secret photographs and escape from someone who is following you.

As well as puzzles and games to play, you will also find information about real-life spies and their spying techniques.

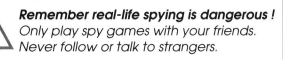

> ⚠️ **Remember real-life spying is dangerous !**
> *Only play spy games with your friends.*
> *Never follow or talk to strangers.*

WHAT YOU NEED

On these pages you can see the things
you need to make a complete spy kit and to play
the games in the book.

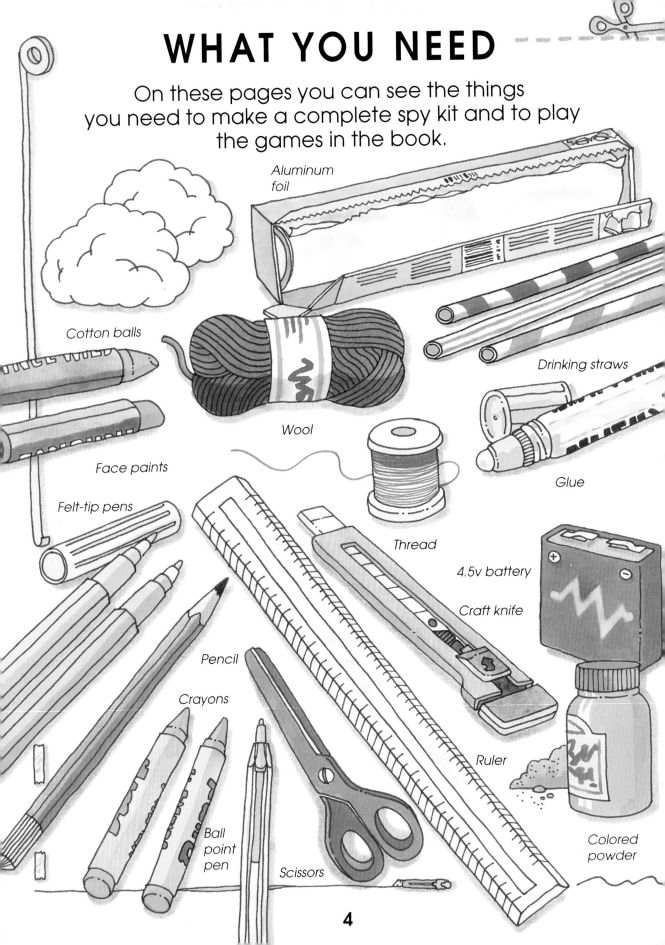

Aluminum foil

Cotton balls

Wool

Drinking straws

Face paints

Felt-tip pens

Thread

Glue

4.5v battery

Craft knife

Pencil

Crayons

Ruler

Ball point pen

Scissors

Colored powder

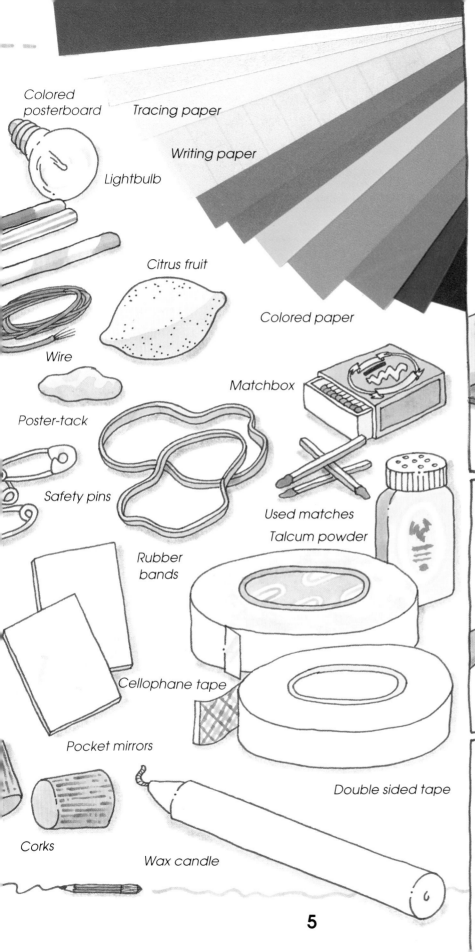

Colored posterboard

Tracing paper

Writing paper

Lightbulb

Citrus fruit

Colored paper

Wire

Matchbox

Poster-tack

Safety pins

Used matches

Talcum powder

Rubber bands

Cellophane tape

Pocket mirrors

Double sided tape

Corks

Wax candle

For safety, always tilt the cutting edge of the blade away from you and cut past your body. Place what you are cutting on a workboard, or a thick piece of cardboard.

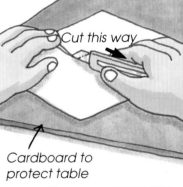

Cut this way

Cardboard to protect table

Scoring

Run the point of an empty ball point pen firmly along lines you want to fold.

Press down hard

REMEMBER

Anything sharp or hot can harm you. When you see this danger sign, ask an adult to help you.

DISGUISES

A spy must not be recognized. Here are some ways to change how ~~up a code~~ you look. You could think ~~name, too.~~

You could add a band of paper for hiding secret messages in.

False beards and moustaches are easy to make.

Make sure your spy hat has a wide brim to hide your face.

Coats with high collars help hide your face.

False beard

 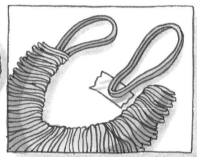

1 Cut a crescent shape out of brown, black, or grey material or paper to fit your face.

2 Glue on strands of black, brown or grey wool, fake fur or cotton wool.

3 Tape or glue rubber bands or loops of string to the ends of the beard and place over your ears.

Collect different hats, old clothes, shoes and scarves for dressing up. Borrow them, or buy them at garage sales and thrift shops.

Change your hairstyle or wear a wig.

Talcum powder rubbed into your hair will make it grey if you are dark or white if you are fair.

Use face paints or makeup to draw on freckles, lines or wrinkles.

Wear sunglasses or the frames of old glasses.

False moustache and eyebrows

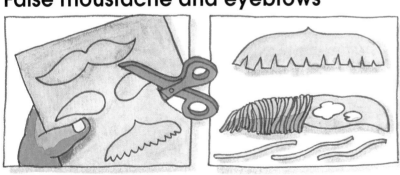

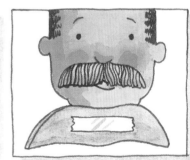

1 Draw a moustache and eyebrows on a piece of paper. Cut them out.

2 Glue on wool, fake fur or cotton balls. Or cut slits into the paper to make it look bushy.

3 Fix them onto your face with double-sided tape.

CODES

A good way to pass on secret information is to write it in a code. Even if your message falls into enemy hands, it will stay a secret!

Line and dot code

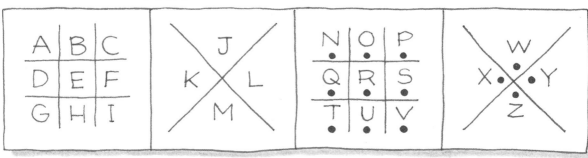

1 Copy these grids onto paper or posterboard. Your friend will need a copy too, to decode your message.

2 You could copy each grid onto a separate piece of paper and tape them together so they can be easily folded to carry in your pocket.

3 Look at the lines and dots on the grids. Instead of writing a letter of the alphabet, just use the lines and dots around it. So, A is ⌐, D is ⊐, and W is ⋁.

Can you work out what this message is?

You could keep your codes hidden in a small matchbox or tin.

Window code

A simple way of sending short messages up to 20 letters in length.

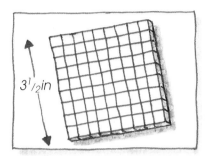

1 Cut out a square of paper or posterboard, 3¹/₂in by 3¹/₂in. Rule lines across and down it at ¹/₂in intervals.

2 Use a craft knife to cut out small squares - the same number as there are letters in your message.

3 Place the square on a piece of blank paper. Write your message, one letter in each hole, reading across and down.

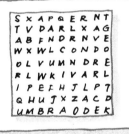

4 Remove the square and fill in the blank spaces on the paper with any letters so your message is hidden.

5 When the square is put back over the letters, the message stands out clearly.

6 Pass the cut-out square to your contact, or make an identical square for them.

Hidden letters

You can hide a secret message in a letter. For example, you could use the first and last letter in each sentence to spell it out. Or you could use the first or last words of each sentence.

Can you find the message in this letter?

It will take some practice to make the letter sound natural.

Meet Sarah at school after seeing me. Joe's friend Nic likes going to the café. 5o'clock is the best time for swimming tonight.

HIDDEN MESSAGES

Messages must be properly hidden or they may be found by enemy spies. Here are some ideas for hiding places.

*Inside your hat
(or tuck it in the hat band)*

*In a chewing-gum pack
(offer your contact a
stick of gum)*

*Rolled up in
an umbrella
(say goodbye
to your contact
and take his
or her identical
umbrella)*

*Inside a book
("accidentally" leave
it behind on a bench
for your contact
to pick up)*

*In a newspaper
("throw away" the
newspaper in a
garbage can)*

Spying on spies!

Arrange to meet your contact and pass on the message or leave it in a dead-letter box - a hiding place such as a hollow tree or a garbage can.

How many hiding places can you see in the picture?

In your shoe (while pretending to tie your shoe lace, slip the message from your shoe under a stone)

Make a secret badge

Put a secret message inside!

1 Cut out two posterboard circles the same size. Glue a $^1/_4$in wide strip of posterboard around the edge of one circle.

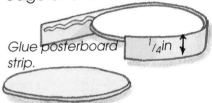

Glue posterboard strip. $^1/_4$in

2 Draw and cut out shapes. Glue them to the front of the same circle. Attach the other circle to the back with a piece of tape. The front of the badge should lift off like a lid.

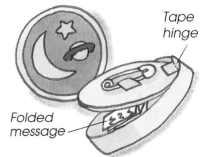

Tape hinge

Folded message

3 Tape a safety pin to the back. Place your message inside, close up the badge and pin it on.

STUN GAME

Real spies are constantly in danger of being discovered and captured by the enemy. They must guard against spycatchers!

Stun dart game

Play this game with a friend and stun the enemy spies.

You need:
Corks
Poster-tack
Used matches
Glue
Drinking straws

⚠️ **DO NOT FIRE DARTS AT PEOPLE**

Make 6 stun darts each.

1 To make a stun dart, stick a small piece of poster-tack on the end of a used matchstick. Roll it between your fingers so that it fits inside the straw to fire the dart.

2 For two teams of spies, trace onto thin cardboard two sets of the figures on page 13. Color and cut them out.

3 Draw a number on the back of each figure. See the scoring details opposite for which numbers to use.

4 Cut a slot in the top of the corks and glue a figure in each one.

How to play

1 Each player is a spycatcher who must try to stun the spies in the enemy team by knocking them over.

2 Arrange the two teams of spies at opposite ends of a table.

3 Take turns shooting at each other's spies. To stun a spy, you must knock it over.

4 When you have used all your darts, add up the numbers on the backs of the spies you have stunned to find your scores. The person with the highest score is the winner.

Scoring

Each team is led by one Master Spy, worth 10 points.

Each team has a Double-Agent worth 5 points. If you hit the Double-Agent, you double your total score.

The rest of your spies should be numbered 1, 2, 3 and 4.

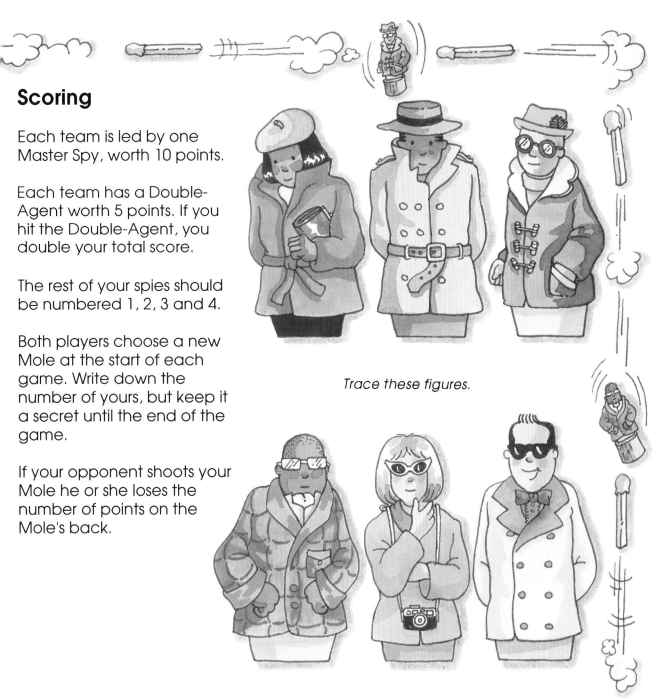

Trace these figures.

Both players choose a new Mole at the start of each game. Write down the number of yours, but keep it a secret until the end of the game.

If your opponent shoots your Mole he or she loses the number of points on the Mole's back.

13

SECRET WRITING

Fool your enemies by writing invisible messages. Make sure your friends know how to make them reappear.

Invisible ink

Orange, lemon and grapefruit juices make the best inks. You could also try potato juice, onion juice or milk.

You could sharpen the matchstick in a pencil sharpener.

Store the juice in a clean, empty jar or bottle with a lid.

1 Cut the fruit in half and squeeze out the juice. An egg cup makes a good container.

2 Dip a used matchstick into the juice and use it to write a message.

3 When the juice dries, the writing will have vanished.

Remember to add a clue to show there is an invisible message.

Write your message in between the lines of an ordinary letter.

The message reappears in clear, brown writing.

ASK AN ADULT TO HELP

4 To read the message heat the paper on the top shelf of a cool oven at 300°F. Check it every few minutes so it doesn't get too hot.

ty

ou had a good the seaside with

ed. Did you buy

ck for me and

says she

Dear Aunty

Meet me at the

I hope you had

Magic pencil

Destroy this page!

1 Write a message with a pencil or pen on a notepad. Press hard so it leaves marks on the next page.

2 The outlines should show up faintly on the next page.

3 To read the message, scribble gently all over the page with a pencil. The writing will show up white.

Wax writing

1 Wax some paper by rubbing it with a candle or crayon. Lay the waxed side on plain paper.

2 Press hard when writing your secret message so that it prints in wax marks on the plain paper.

3 To read the message, sprinkle colored powder over it. The powder will stick to the message but slide off the rest of the paper.

For colored powder you could use instant powdered coffee, colored chalk scrapings or dry powder paint.

LOOKING AND LISTENING

Real spies use special equipment to help them listen secretly to conversations, and to keep a hidden watch on people. You can make your own "spywatch" equipment.

Bugs

A bug has a tiny microphone inside it. If it is hidden in a room, a spy outside can overhear conversations.

A plastic bottle cap covered with foil makes a realistic-looking bug.

You could disguise your bugs by making them look like insects or sweets.

Fill your bug with poster-tack so that it sticks easily to surfaces. Or tape a little magnet to it for sticking on metal surfaces.

Spider bug - pipecleaner legs

Licorice bug

Candy bug - disguised in an old candy wrapper

Flower bug - paper petals

Ladybird bug - paper spotted wings

Fly bug - plastic wings

Hiding place

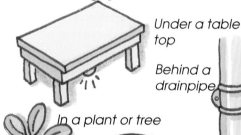

Under a table top

Behind a drainpipe

In a plant or tree

Under a phone

Bugged !

 1 Throw a die. The player who scores highest hides the bugs.

2 The other players leave the room and count to 100.

3 The players return to the room and look for the bugs. Set a time limit - perhaps 5 minutes.

4 The player who finds the most bugs hides them in the next round.

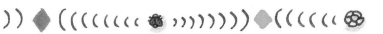

Periscope

Use a periscope for looking around corners, or for spying over a wall or fence.

You need :

Piece of cardboard
8in x 23¹/₄in or an
empty aluminum foil
or plastic wrap
2 pocket mirrors
Scissors
Rubber bands
pencil and ruler

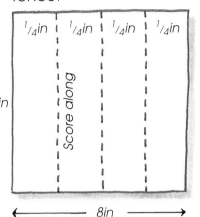

¹/₄in   ¹/₄in   ¹/₄in   ¹/₄in

Score along

←————— 8in —————→

1 Draw three lines 2in apart along the cardboard as shown. Score along the lines so you can bend the cardboard.

2 Draw two lines across, 2¹/₄in from the top and bottom. Cut out the squares shown in the drawing below.

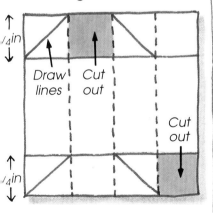

Draw lines   Cut out

Cut out

3 Draw lines diagonally across the four squares shown in the diagram.

4 Bend the cardboard around to make a tube. Fasten rubber bands around each end. Place a mirror at each end, using the diagonal lines you drew as a guide.

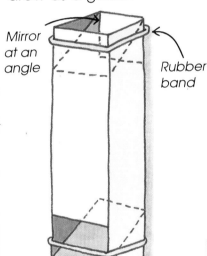

Mirror at an angle

Rubber band

Adjust the angle of the mirrors until when you hold the periscope just above a wall or fence, you can see something reflected from the top mirror into the bottom mirror.

If the mirrors drop out, fasten the rubber bands more tightly.

You could add paper leaves to camouflage your periscope.

SENDING SIGNALS

In a dangerous situation, it may be best to signal an urgent message. Make a Morse Code flasher and send for help fast !

Morse flasher

You need :

*4.5 volt battery with flat metal connecting strips
Lightbulb
Strip of cardboard folded in two
Matchbox
2 x 8in long wires
Poster-tack, cellophane tape, aluminum foil*

1 Bare about $1\frac{1}{4}$in of the ends of the wires.

2 Wrap the ends of the 8in-long wires around the connecting strips of the battery. Fasten with tape.

3 Wrap the other end of one of the longer wires around the bulb. Tape the end of the shorter wire to the base of the bulb. Secure with tape or poster-tack.

4 Wrap a piece of foil around the free end of the other long wire. Stick it to the cardboard strip with poster-tack.

5 Wrap foil around the free end of the short wire and stick it to the other end of the cardboard strip.

6 Press the folded cardboard strip down so the pieces of foil touch. The bulb will light up.

Cut holes in the ends of a matchbox for the bulb and wires to go through.

If the bulb doesn't light, make sure all the connections are firmly fixed.

How to send a Morse Code message

This is the Morse Code. Each letter of the alphabet is a different arrangement of dots and dashes. To flash your Morse Code message, make short flashes for dots and long ones for dashes.

- ● Short flash
- ▬ Long flash

A	B	C	D	E	F
● ▬	▬ ● ● ●	▬ ● ▬ ●	▬ ● ●	●	● ● ▬ ●
G	**H**	**I**	**J**	**K**	**L**
▬ ▬ ●	● ● ● ●	● ●	● ▬ ▬ ▬	▬ ● ▬	● ▬ ● ●
M	**N**	**O**	**P**	**Q**	**R**
▬ ▬	▬ ●	▬ ▬ ▬	● ▬ ▬ ●	▬ ▬ ● ▬	● ▬ ●
S	**T**	**U**	**V**	**W**	**X**
● ● ●	▬	● ● ▬	● ● ● ▬	● ▬ ▬	▬ ● ● ▬
Y	**Z**				
▬ ● ▬ ▬	▬ ▬ ● ●				

Make your own signals

Flash messages with a mirror or a flashlight: two flashes for danger, three for all clear.

Flashlight

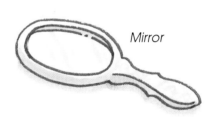
Mirror

Body language

Make up signals: for example, rubbing your nose could mean "Meet me later."

Scratching your ear - "I'll telephone you later."

Rubbing your eyes - "Be careful, you're being watched."

Scratching your head - "Don't do anything."

Hands behind back - "I can't pass a message now."

One hand in pocket - "Yes."

Two hands in pockets - "No."

19

TRICKS AND SKILLS

To outwit the enemy, a clever spy must know all kinds of tricks and skills. Here are some important ones.

Spy-traps

How do you know if an enemy agent has goten into your room? Here are some ways to make it spy-proof.

If someone opens the door the hair will break.

If someone comes in, the box will fall.

Tape the thread low down.

Glue a hair across a door or drawer. When you return, check to see if it is still there.

Tape thread onto a small open box. Fill it with rice or flour. Tape the other end to the door. Balance the box on the door frame.

Tape a thin cotton thread across a door opening or between two walls. It will fall down if someone walks through it.

Mark the position of furniture and objects in your room with chalk marks. Then you will be able to tell if anything has been moved.

Sprinkle talcum powder on the floor. An intruder's footprints will show up clearly.

Remember to ask an adult's permission before setting any of these spy traps

Shake off a tail

Try these tricks with a friend tailing (following) you.

Carry a quick disguise. Dash into a doorway and walk out looking different.

Head for a crowd. It will keep you hidden from view.

Suddenly turn and face your "tail". If he or she turns and walks away, run down a side street.

Keep changing direction. Take a zig-zag route or go the longest way around.

Turn a corner, sit down on a bench and hide your face in a newspaper until your "tail" has passed.

Make a dummy

If you think you are being watched by someone outside the house, make a dummy by putting your clothes around pillows and propping them up. Seat it near a window. Slip out of the back door and leave your enemy to keep an eye on it!

SPYWATCH

Governments send up satellites and planes into the sky to take photographs to find out information about other countries.

Hidden camera

A camera can be a very useful part of a spy's equipment for collecting important evidence. You may have your own camera. If not, you could borrow one or buy one of the cheap "throwaway" cameras now available.

There are lots of ways you can hide your camera and yourself so that no one knows you are taking photographs.

Roll down the car window as you drive past.

Hide your camera under your coat until the last moment.

Keep your camera hidden in a bag.

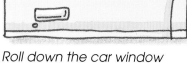

Hide yourself behind a newspaper and cut a small hole in it for your camera lens to peep through.

Pretend to be taking a photo in another direction, then swing around.

Hide behind or in a tree!

Simon Spyman's photos

Here is a photo taken by Simon Spyman. See if you can spot any suspicious goings-on.

Spy plane

Make model spy planes with your friends and fly them over each other's territory.

You need :
Pencil
Used matchsticks
Rubber bands

Colored posterboard
Colored paper
Glue
Scissors

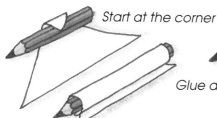

Start at the corner

Glue down edge

Cut at an angle

1 Cut out a triangle with sides the same length as your pencil. Roll it around the pencil to make the body of the plane.

2 Glue the edge down and slide the pencil out.

3 Squeeze and glue one end down. Cut it at an angle to make the nose of the plane.

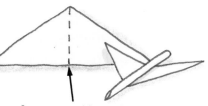

Score and bend up

About 1¹/₂in slit

Glue matchstick at an angle

4 Use a triangle of posterboard for the wings. Score and bend along the middle and across the wingtips. Glue to the body.

5 Cut out a tail fin. Make a slit at the tail end of the body, slide the tail fin in and glue.

6 Make a hole under the nose and glue in a matchstick at an angle.

Flying the plane

Hook a rubber band over the matchstick. Pull the tail fin back in one hand and pull the elastic band in front with the other. Let go of the plane and watch it fly !

If the plane swoops up too high, bend the wingtips down.

If the plane dives, bend the wingtips up more.

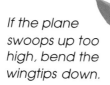

Spy plane game

Lay large squares of different colored paper on the ground for territories. If you fly your plane over another person's territory, win 5 points. If you land on their territory, win 10 points.

SPY MAZE

← Spy

The blue-coated spy in the basement of the castle has the secret plans. Can you help him find a way through the maze and out of the castle before the yellow-coated spycatchers close in on him?

SPY FACTS

Devices and gadgets

Here are some of the hi-tec devices and gadgets that spies use today. Many of them are used for spying on business meetings (called industrial espionage.)

Pen transmitter (bug) : *records conversations over 328ft away.*

Digital voice changer: *a microphone that fits over the mouthpiece of a telephone and disguises voices by making men's voices sound like women's, and women's sound like men's.*

Earspy: *a tiny electronic device that fits in the ear and receives messages from a contact. A miniature microphone (hidden under a jacket lapel or tie) enables the spy to reply.*

Telephone transmitter (bug): *a tiny recording device which is hidden in the telephone and starts recording both sides of the conversation as soon as someone speaks.*

Video briefcase: *a special briefcase containing a miniature video camera with a lens the size of a pinhole. It can be turned on by changing the briefcase's combination lock.*

"Antenna" camera: *it looks like an ordinary car antenna, but hidden inside is a tiny camera lens. The rest of the camera is hidden under the bodywork.*

Bug detector: *an electronic "sweeping" device that detects and locates bugs.*

Night vision goggles: *enable you to see clearly in the dark.*

Laser bugging: *a laser beam is aimed at a window and picks up conversations by analyzing the minute vibrations of the glass made by the sound of voices.*

Famous spy stories

In 500 BC, a greek spy went on a long journey to deliver a message. It was perfectly hidden – tattooed on his head! It could be read only when his hair was shaved off.

Lord Baden-Powell, founder of the Boy Scout movement, spent months learning about butterflies so he could go on an army mission disguised as a butterfly collector. He sketched details of enemy weapons into the patterns of butterfly wings he was drawing.

Mata Hari, a Dutch woman, was a famous spy during World War 1. Her real name was Gertrud Zelle. She became a dancer in Paris, and worked for both the German and

Charles Eon de Beaumont was a French spy who lived in the eighteenth century. He was sent on a mission to a Russian court disguised as a woman. He was so successful that the Russian empress actually made him her maid of honor.

French Secret Services. She was not a very good spy and was not loyal to either side. Eventually she was arrested by the French and shot by firing squad.

Worldwide intelligence services

Most countries have an intelligence service. Their job is usually to collect information secretly about what is happening in other countries. Here are a few of them:

CIA USA's Central Intelligence Agency
FBI USA's spy-catching organization
MI6 Britain's international Secret Service
MI5 Britain's mainland Secret Service, working closely with the Special Branch of the police force.
KGB Secret Service of the former Soviet Union
ASIO Australian Secret Intelligence Organization
BOSS South Africa's intelligence service
CESID Spain's intelligence service
CSIS Canadian Security Intelligence Service

SPY WORDS

Bug A tiny hidden listening device.

Burnt A word used to describe a spy who has been discovered by the enemy.

Cobbler A forger of passports.

Code-name The name a spy is known by.

Contact A member of a spy ring or group.

Dead-letter box A place to hide messages.

Decode To work out a coded message.

Double-agent A spy working for two countries at the same time.

Drop To leave a message for another spy.

Encode To put a message into code.

Espionage Another word for spying.

Fix To blackmail.

Going private To leave the Secret Service.

Hospital Prison.

Intelligence Information.

Master spy The head of a spy ring.

Mole A spy who joins the enemy to steal their secrets.

Pavement artist A spy keeping watch on a house.

Peep A spy photographer.

Piano study Radio operating.

Plant To hide something secretly, such as a bug.

Playback When a spy is caught and forced to send false information.

Plumbing Preparation for a major operation.

Safe house A hideaway.

Secret agent Another name for a spy.

Shadowing Secretly following the enemy.

Shoe A false passport.

Spycatcher A spy who traps enemy spies.

Spy ring A team of spies.

Stroller A spy using a walkie-talkie.

Tail A spy who follows another.

Thirty-threes An emergency.

Turned agent A spy who leaves to work for the other side.

Undercover Working in disguise.

What's your twenty? Where exactly are you?

DID YOU KNOW?

• The first recorded use of spies in history is in the Bible. Moses sent some Israelites into Canaan to see if it was safe to enter.

• Samurai warriors from Japan were sometimes trained as spies. They were called Ninjas.

• In 1986 two spies were caught sending messages from a garden shed at their home in Cranford, England.

Part 2

Detectives

CONTENTS

ABOUT THIS BOOK

Detectives find out all they can about crimes that have been committed. They search for clues, talk to witnesses, and collect as much information as they can.

In this book, Detective Dan pieces together the puzzle of the jewels stolen from Oakwood Hall. You can help him solve the crime, and make a detective kit of your own to play with.

Step-by-step instructions show you how to make a fingerprint kit for collecting and identifying prints at the scene of the crime. You can also find out how to disguise yourself when you are on the trail of a suspect, test a witness's story with a lie-detector machine, and make a pair of handcuffs to arrest the crimal!

There are tips on how to read body language, and games to sharpen your powers of observation and memory.

You will also find out about the first real detectives, famous storybook detectives, and how science helps today's detectives to solve crimes.

 Remember that being a detective is dangerous !
Only play detective games with your friends.
Never follow or talk to strangers.

WHAT YOU NEED

On these pages you can see the things you need to make a complete detective kit and to play the games in the book.

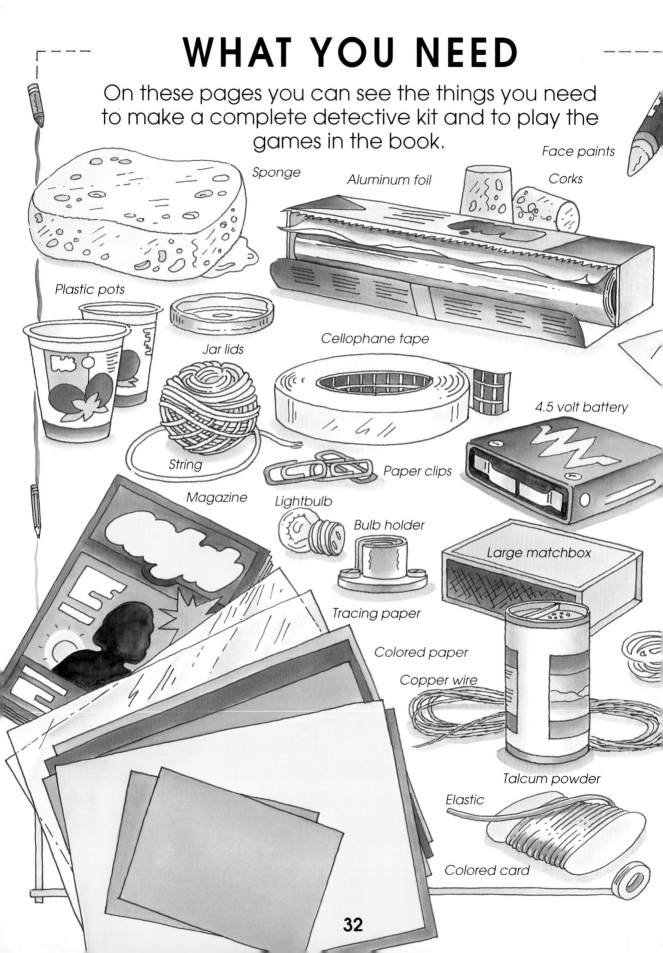

Sponge

Aluminum foil

Face paints

Corks

Plastic pots

Jar lids

Cellophane tape

4.5 volt battery

String

Paper clips

Magazine

Lightbulb

Bulb holder

Large matchbox

Tracing paper

Colored paper

Copper wire

Talcum powder

Elastic

Colored card

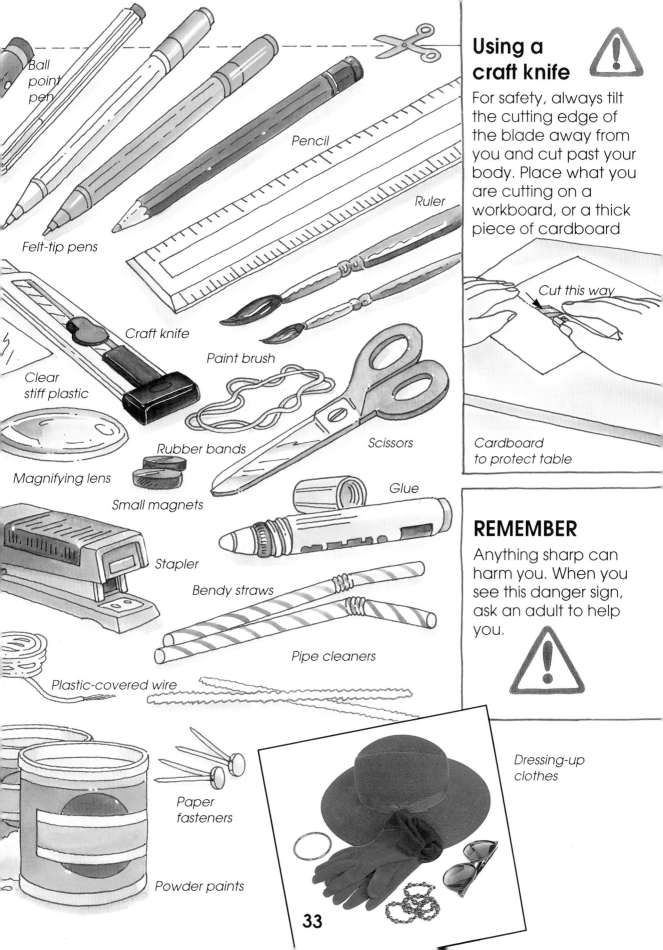

Ball point pen

Pencil

Felt-tip pens

Ruler

Craft knife

Paint brush

Clear stiff plastic

Rubber bands

Scissors

Magnifying lens

Small magnets

Glue

Stapler

Bendy straws

Pipe cleaners

Plastic-covered wire

Paper fasteners

Powder paints

Dressing-up clothes

Using a craft knife

For safety, always tilt the cutting edge of the blade away from you and cut past your body. Place what you are cutting on a workboard, or a thick piece of cardboard

Cut this way

Cardboard to protect table

REMEMBER

Anything sharp can harm you. When you see this danger sign, ask an adult to help you.

33

THE CASE

The phone rings in Detective Dan's office. He hurries to answer it - perhaps it is another exciting case.

"It's Lady Oakwood," says the voice on the phone. "The family jewels have been stolen!" "I'll be there right away!" says Dan, picking up his ID badge and his warrant card.

Detectives carry identification to show who they are. Make a warrant card like Dan's, giving your name, rank and photograph, and an ID (identity) badge. To make the warrant card, first cut out a $3^1/_2$in by $2^1/_4$in piece of stiff cardboard and round off the corners.

Warrant card

Colored cardboard

Make a baage from paper or cardboard and glue it on.

$2^1/_4$in

$3^1/_2$in

EDWARD JONES

E Jones

Write your name and official detective signature here.

Glue on a square of white paper. Stick a smaller square of colored paper on top.

Glue your picture here.

Cover the front of the card with clear plastic.

Staple the edges together or make a tape border.

Use a passport-sized photo or drawing.

Make an ID badge

An identity (ID) badge can be worn secretly inside your coat when you go investigating.

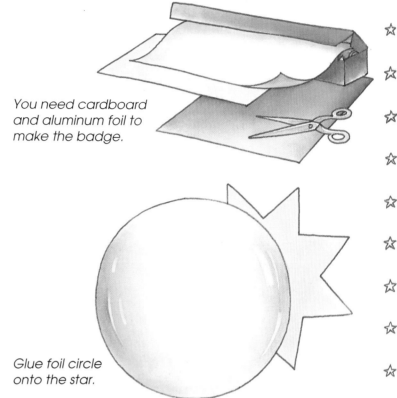

You need cardboard and aluminum foil to make the badge.

Glue foil circle onto the star.

1 Trace this star onto cardboard and cut it out.

2 Cut a foil circle to fit the star. Glue it on to the star.

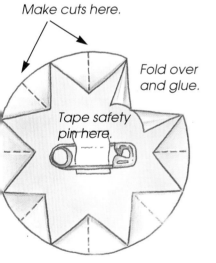

Make cuts here.

Fold over and glue.

Tape safety pin here.

Use an empty pen to score patterns on the star.

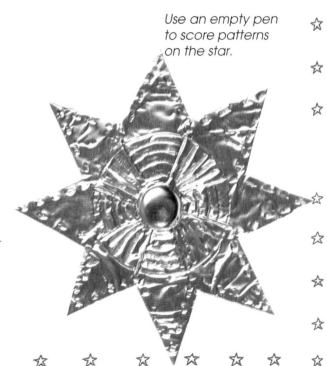

3 Glue back the foil edges as shown. Tape a safety pin to the back of the badge.

You could stick a paper fastener through the middle.

SCENE OF THE CRIME

Dan soon arrives at Oakwood Hall to investigate the case of the missing jewels. He is greeted by Lord Oakwood's new wife, Lady Fenella Oakwood.

Part 1

Lady Oakwood leads Detective Dan to the scene of the crime. The room is a mess. Chairs are knocked over, a window is broken and the wall safe that once contained the jewels is wide open.

Dan looks around him carefully, thinking about what he sees. Then he begins to dust for fingerprints.

The safe was not forced open.

Why are the chairs knocked over and the drawers pulled open?

If the thief got in through the window, why is there no broken glass inside the room?

Taking fingerprints

Keep a record of people's fingerprints - you may need to check them against any you find at the scene of the crime.

1 Press a suspect's fingertip on an ink pad and then onto paper so it leaves a print.

2 Take a print from each of their fingers and thumbs. Label the prints with the owner's name and glue them in a notebook.

Fingerprint kit

Everyone has his or her own fingerprint pattern. Nobody else will have fingerprints exactly the same as yours. That is why prints can be helpful clues. Use this kit to take the fingerprints of suspects and to identify any prints found at the scene of a crime.

Magnifying lens for studying and identifying fingerprints.

Make an ink pad

When not in use, cover sponge with another jar lid.

1 Cut a piece of sponge to fit inside a jar lid.

2 Make "ink" from paint and water and soak sponge.

Fingerprint powder

Powder is dusted onto things to make any fingerprints on them show up. Use darker powder on light things and light powder on dark things.

Make dark powder by grinding a pencil against the blade of a sharpener. Or use dry black powder paint.

Keep powders in a matchbox.

Use talcum powder or a powder puff for light powder.

Cellophane tape for collecting prints.

Collecting prints

1 Brush powder over door handles, glasses, cups – wherever you might find prints. **Ask an adult's permission first !**

2 Make "ink" from paint and water and soak sponge.

3 Press cellophane tape over the print. Peel the tape off, bringing the powdery print with it.

4 Use the magnifying glass to study the print. Does the pattern of lines match any print already in your notebook?

QUESTIONING

To find out what actually happened, Detective Dan interviews Lord and Lady Oakwood and their two guests.

Dan questions them one by one and writes down everything they say in his notebook. He also makes notes about their body language – the way they behave under questioning.

Lord Anthony Oakwood

Upset and shocked. Saw and heard nothing.

Lady Fenella Oakwood

Discovered the theft. Calm and dignified. Saw and heard nothing.

Rupert Wright

Engaged to Laura Mackenzie. Rather nervous. Kept biting his lip. Saw and heard nothing.

Laura Mackenzie

Friend of Lady Oakwood. Engaged to Rupert Wright. Blushed and fiddled with her hair. Heard glass breaking in the night.

Make a notebook

Make your own detective notebook and use it to note down any clues you find. Keep a record, too, of what people say during interviews.

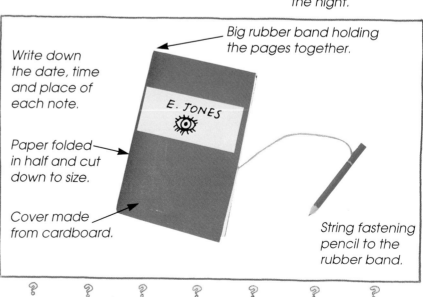

Write down the date, time and place of each note.

Big rubber band holding the pages together.

E. JONES

Paper folded in half and cut down to size.

Cover made from cardboard.

String fastening pencil to the rubber band.

Interviewing

Interview each person separately. Ask them questions. Keep notes of what they say. Study the way they behave to see if they are being honest with you.

Don't forget that a hardened criminal may be very good at deceiving you, and an innocent person may look guilty just because he or she is frightened!

Does everyone agree about the incident?

Does anybody give answers that contradict what the others say?

Does anybody's behavior seem suspicious?

Biting lips: May be afraid of saying too much.

Biting nails or fiddling with fingers: Nervous.

Twiddling with clothes or face: Nervous.

Hands on hips, turning away from you: Defiant and aggressive.

Crossed arms or legs: The person is defensive. He or she may not be telling you everything.

Hands held open with palms upwards: Open and honest.

Leaning towards you with hands clenched : Aggressive and maybe angry.

Lying

If somebody begins to do any of these things while speaking, it suggests they may be lying. Then you could try the lie detector test on p. 50.

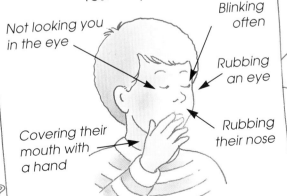

Not looking you in the eye

Blinking often

Rubbing an eye

Covering their mouth with a hand

Rubbing their nose

Observation game

If you are on a bus or train, try to guess the age, occupation and character of some of the passengers. You could even invent a name for them and write a story around their characters.

39

IDENTIKIT

Next day, Laura Mackenzie - Lady Oakwood's friend - calls to see Detective Dan. She has some important information for him.

Part 3

"I've just remembered something," says Laura. "There was a man – a stranger – near Oakwood Hall the day before the burglary."

" Can you describe him?" asks Dan. To jog her memory, Dan shows her the faces in his identikit file. At last they put together a picture of the stranger.

Different faces

To begin to build up an identikit picture you need to know general details such as the shape of the person's face and coloring.

Then you add details of the person's features, such as nose, eyes and mouth.

Oval face
Round face
Square face

Red hair
Reddish coloring

Dark hair
Brown skin

Blonde hair
Pale skin

Large ears

Brown eyes

Small mouth

Pointed ears

Big mouth

Small nose

Large eyes

Long nose

Brown eyes

Small round ears

Thin mouth

Big nose

Make an identikit book

Detectives build up pictures of a suspect's face by using witnesses' reports and identikit files.

Identikit files contain hundreds of pictures of different faces. The witness puts together different features, until the whole face looks like the suspect.

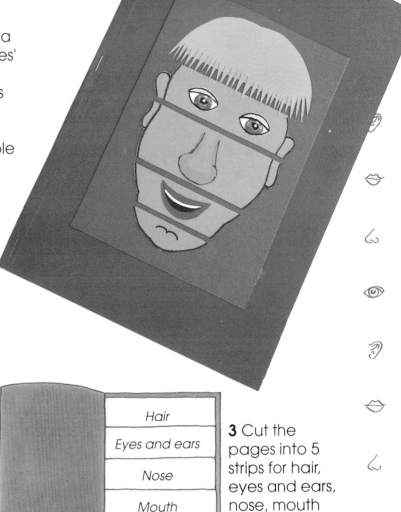

Make your own identikit book to help your investigations.

1 Fold four or more sheets of paper in half. Put them together to make a book.

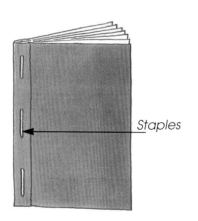

Staples

2 Make a cover from colored paper. Staple the book together.

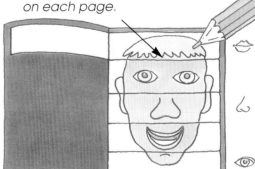

| Hair |
| Eyes and ears |
| Nose |
| Mouth |
| Chin |

3 Cut the pages into 5 strips for hair, eyes and ears, nose, mouth and chin.

Draw a different type of face on each page.

4 Draw a face on the first page. Turn back the strips and draw in different hair, eyes, noses, etc.

41

COMMUNICATIONS

Detective Dan is looking for clues in the grounds of Oakwood Hall.

He stops outside the summerhouse – there are people talking inside. Putting his ear to the wall, Dan can hear their conversation. He hears a man saying, "I'm meeting him tomorrow in Tony's Café at 4 p.m." At once, Dan telephones back to headquarters.

Part 4

Make a telephone link

This is an amusing telephone. The sound travels along the string and can be heard in the yogurt pot "receiver."

1 Find two empty yogurt pots (or similar plastic containers). Make a hole in the bottom of each.

2 Put one end of a long string into one of the holes and knot it inside the pot.

3 Put the other end of the string into the hole in the other pot and tie a knot inside, as before.

String

Knot inside

4 Stretch the string out until it is taut. Take it in turns to talk into one pot and listen in the other.

How far away can you hear each other?

Make a model radio

Bendy straw

Cardboard "buttons"

Large matchbox

Colored paper

Cellophane tape

Keep a radio hidden on you for passing messages to HQ.

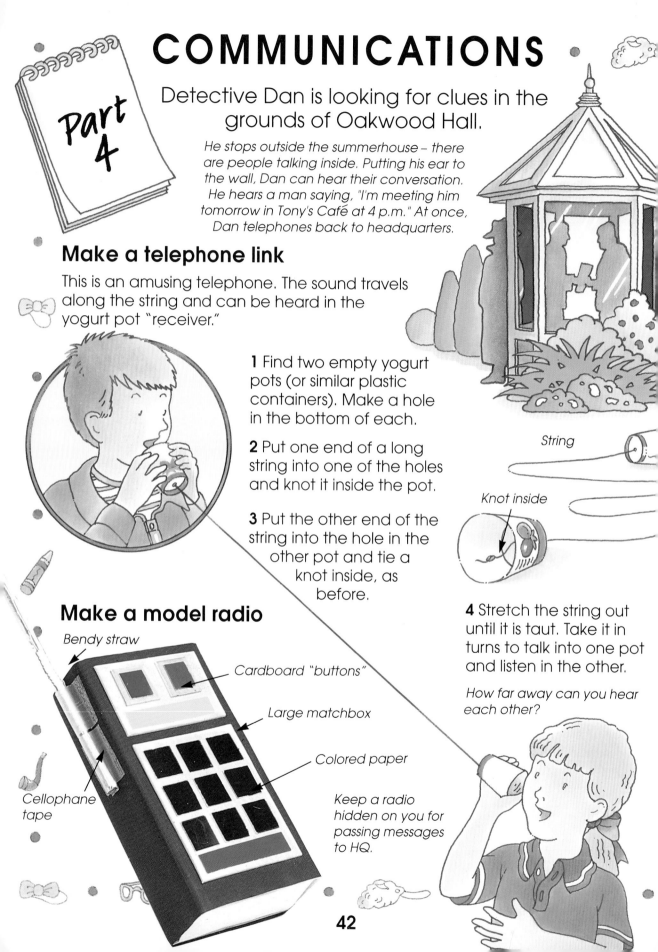

42

DISGUISE

Following the clue he overheard, Dan goes to Tony's Café at 4 p.m. the next day, in disguise.

Rupert Wright comes in and sits at a table with a man whose face seems familiar. Dan watches the men through his special surveillance newspaper. The men swap identical packages and get up to leave. Rupert has dropped a crumpled piece of paper. Dan picks it up – it has a series of numbers on it .

Eyeholes cut in a newspaper help you see without being seen.

Nose and glasses disguise

Fold a piece of thin cardboard in two and trace this shape onto it. Cut it out and open it. Cut out the eye holes.

Cut out and color.

Cut out

Bend back

Fasten elastic here if you wish.

← *Fold*

You can omit the moustache.

Other ideas for disguises

A big hat

Empty frames or sunglasses

Wig or a different hair style

Old clothes

Pillow tied under your clothes to change your shape

Wrinkles made with face paints

43

LOOKING AT CLUES

Detective Dan studies the clues he has collected so far.

Part 6

Suddenly, Dan realizes something important: the person Rupert Wright met in the café is the man in the identikit picture! Dan decides to ask the information section at HQ to help find out who this man is. Then a Spottercopter crew report they have just seen the occupants of Oakwood Hall driving away!

An investigation chart

Back at the office, Dan has made a chart to sum up all the clues he has so far. Pin the evidence from your own investigations to a bulletinboard.

INVESTIGATION
Theft of jewels from Oakwood Hall.

Safe was not forced open. The only fingerprints on the safe door are Lady Oakwood's.

Identikit picture of stranger seen near Oakwood Hall matches man seen with Rupert Wright.

Glass found in windowbox, not in room - window broken from inside.

Numbers dropped by Rupert Wright - are they the combination of the safe?

6 4 15
32 2 0

Main suspect: Rupert Wright.

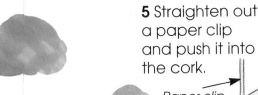

Make a Spottercopter

Here is a fun mobile to make. Hang it in your room to keep watch when you are away!

1 To make the body of the helicopter, cut each end off a bottle cork at an angle, like this:

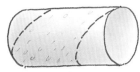

ASK AN ADULT TO HELP YOU CUT THE CORK WITH A CRAFT KNIFE

2 Glue colored paper over it to look like windows and bodywork.

3 To make the tail, cut a strip of colored paper, about $3/4$in wide. Fold it and glue it to the body, trimming it to make it a bit narrower towards the back.

4 To make the rotor, cut out a circle of acetate or other stiff plastic film, about $2^3/4$in across.

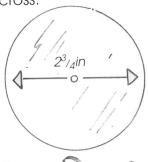

$2^3/4$in

5 Straighten out a paper clip and push it into the cork.

Paper clip

6 Cut a $3/4$in length of drinking straw and fit it over the paper clip. Fix the plastic circle on top.

Drinking straw — *Large circle*

7 Bend the top of the paper clip over into a loop. Hang spottercopter from paper clouds attached to cotton thread and pipecleaner.

8 To make the tail rotor, cut out a small plastic circle and glue a dot of colored cardboard in the center. Glue the plastic circle to the tail.

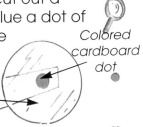

Colored cardboard dot

Tail   *Small circle*

9 Trace this shape and cut it out of cardboard to make the skids. Fold and glue them underneath the body.

Fold

Skids

Fold

OBSERVATION

While everyone is away from Oakwood Hall, Dan looks for further clues around the grounds.

Behind the house, a muddy shovel is leaning against a wall. Some flowers in the garden have been trampled. In the grass he finds a woman's glove. To avoid spoiling the fingerprints on the glove, he picks it up with a stick and puts it in a plastic bag.

Look and remember

Most people remember very little of what they see. Detectives, however, must watch carefully and notice even the smallest details. The observation games shown here will help you develop your detective skills.

Your move!

1 Make model buildings from folded pieces of cardboard or posterboard. Draw on windows and doors, or cut them out of colored paper and glue them on. Cut out trees, cars and figures from cardboard, leaving a base to fold over (you may need to stick them down with poster-tack).

2 Send your friends out of the room. Arrange the houses, cars and people any way you like.

3 Call your friends in again and give them 30 seconds to look at the scene. Then send them out again.

4 Move some pieces or take a few away. Call everyone back in and see who is first to spot all the changes!

Get the picture!

This is a good party game. Cut out a photo from a magazine. Pass it around for people to study for a short time. Then ask questions about it.

Get everyone to write their answers down. Award points for right answers and a prize for the person with the best memory!

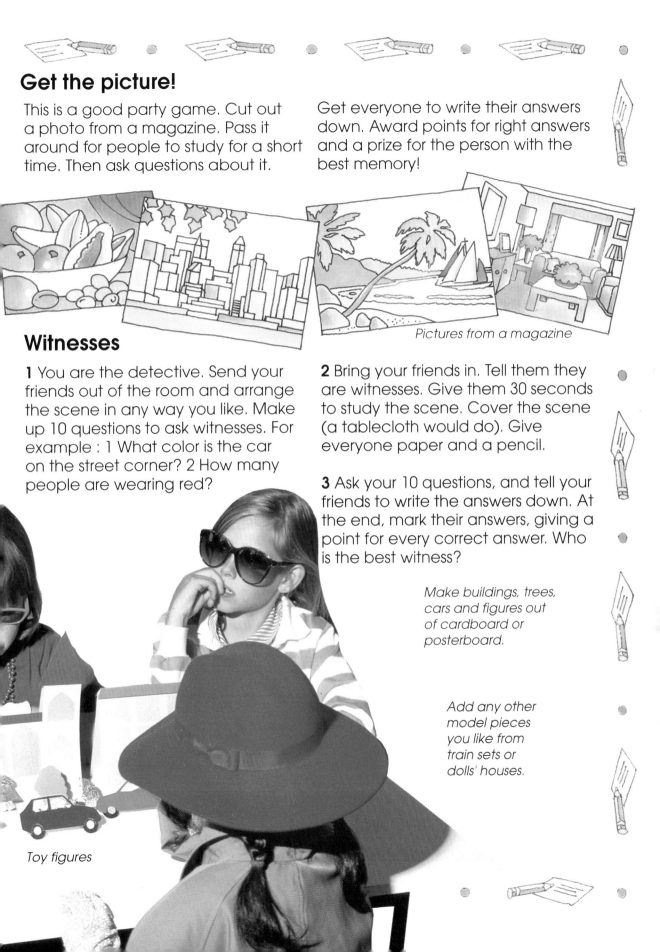

Pictures from a magazine

Witnesses

1 You are the detective. Send your friends out of the room and arrange the scene in any way you like. Make up 10 questions to ask witnesses. For example : 1 What color is the car on the street corner? 2 How many people are wearing red?

2 Bring your friends in. Tell them they are witnesses. Give them 30 seconds to study the scene. Cover the scene (a tablecloth would do). Give everyone paper and a pencil.

3 Ask your 10 questions, and tell your friends to write the answers down. At the end, mark their answers, giving a point for every correct answer. Who is the best witness?

Make buildings, trees, cars and figures out of cardboard or posterboard.

Add any other model pieces you like from train sets or dolls' houses.

Toy figures

ON THE SCENT

Part 8

Detective Dan has a lot on his mind. He's received some new evidence.

Thanks to his researchers at headquarters, Dan knows the name of the stranger in the café. And, at Oakwood Hall, bloodhound Sherlock sniffs the glove and follows the scent trail to the trampled flowerbed. There a package is dug up, wrapped in a silk scarf. There are bank notes inside!

Magnetic bloodhound game

Make a bloodhound for each player and play this seek and score game.

For each dog you will need:
White cardboard, paper
Felt-tip pens
Paper clips
Small magnet
Glue, scissors

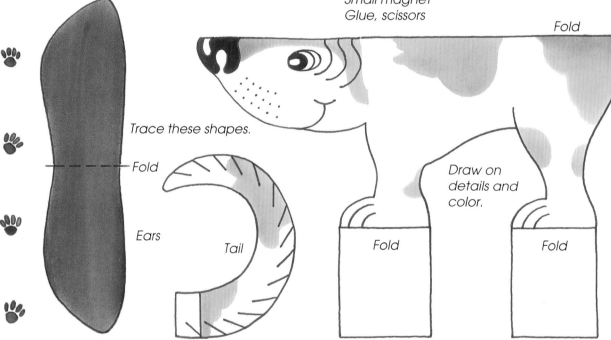

Trace these shapes.

Fold

Ears

Tail

Fold

Fold

Fold

Draw on details and color.

1 Fold a piece of cardboard in two. Trace the dog shape onto it. Cut it out. Do not cut along the fold.

2 Trace the ears and tail onto cardboard. Cut them out and glue them on.

Glue

Glue

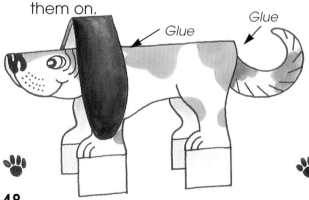

3 Fold the leg flaps and glue them together.

Glue

Glue

4 Glue a small magnet in the bloodhound's nose!

Magnet

You may need to balance the dog with a paper clip on the tail.

To play the game

1 Cut a piece of white paper into at least 20 small pieces.

2 Write a different number on each piece of paper. Use the numbers 1 to 20.

3 Fold each square in half, hiding the number inside. Fasten with a paper clip.

4 Mix all the pieces together on a table top. Take turns pushing your bloodhound out to bring back a piece of paper. (The paper clip will be attracted to the magnet.)

5 When the dog brings the paper "home", open it and look at the number inside. That is your score! When the dogs have picked up all the pieces of paper, add up your scores.

The dog whose owner scores highest is the winner.

THE TRUTH TEST

Now Dan is sure he knows who the real culprit is.
But he has to prove it.

Part 9

The glove and scarf found in the garden turn out to belong to Laura Mackenzie. Dan suspects that Rupert Wright was paid to steal the jewels and that Laura, his fiancée, helped him by burying the money he received for doing it. To find out the truth, he questions Rupert using a lie detector.

Q: Did you fake the break-in at Oakwood Hall and steal the jewels?
A: No! (Bulb flashes – a lie)

Q: So you did do it. Was the payment for the robbery?
A: (Reluctantly) Yes.

Q: Did someone tell you the safe's combination number?
A: No! (Bulb flashes)

Q: Another lie. Was it Lady Oakwood?
A: Yes. I admit it.
"I'm arresting you," says Dan. "You'll be charged at the police station."

Do lie detectors work?

Real lie-detector machines measure changes in pulse rate, blood pressure and breathing that may happen to a suspect under questioning. But, as these machines can be unreliable, they are not used in many countries. However, here is a fun one for you to make and play with.

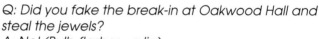

Make a tremblometer

Find out how steady a suspect's hands are under questioning. The tremblometer may help you detect a lie!

You need:
4.5 volt battery
Lightbulb and bulb holder
1 x 8in and 1 x 15³/₄in lengths
 of plastic covered wire
1 x 23¹/₂in length of
 copper wire

Bare the ends of the plastic wires about 1¹/₄in with pliers or scissors.

Wire strippers

1¹/₄in

Bend the copper wire as shown. Fix one end to a battery connector. You might need to tape this down to hold it tight.

Fix one end of this wire to the other battery connector. Screw the other end to one of the bulb holder connectors.

Copper wire

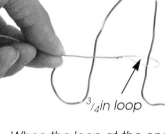

³/₄in loop

When the loop at the end of the wire touches the copper wire, the bulb will flash.

Screw Bulb

Screw

Screw this wire to the other bulb holder connector. Make a ³/₄in loop at the other end of the wire.

Bulb holder

If the bulb doesn't light up, check all the connections are firm.

How to play

Here are some games to play with your friends and your tremblometer!

Steady nerves!
See who can pass the loop along the wire fastest without making the bulb light up!

Truth or lie?
Take turns being the detective, asking questions. The suspect must pass the loop along the wire when they reply. If they are lying, their hand may begin to shake, causing the bulb to light up. Of course, their hand may shake if they are simply nervous!

ARREST!

Dan hears that Lady Oakwood and a man are at the airport. He rushes there and meets them just as they are about to board a plane.

Part 10

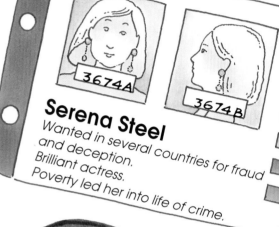

Serena Steel
Wanted in several countries for fraud and deception.
Brilliant actress.
Poverty led her into life of crime.

At the airport Dan arrests and handcuffs Lady Fenella Oakwood, whose real name he now knows is Serena Steel. Dan also arrests her accomplice Hans Zubinsky - the stranger in the café. He was recognized from the identikit picture, and the information about him provided by HQ had included a photograph of his partner - international jewel thief, Serena Steel. Dan had recognized her at once.

To get their hands on the Oakwood jewels, Serena Steel and Hans Zubinsky had worked out a cruel plan. Serena tricked Lord Oakwood into marrying her. Then she invited her friend Laura Mackenzie, with Laura's fiancé Rupert Wright, to stay. Rupert agreed to fake the burglary for a large payment. He then handed over the jewels to Hans, who tried to escape the country with Serena.

How to make handcuffs

Make these fun handcuffs and use them when you play detective games.

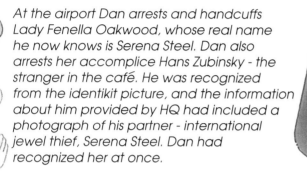

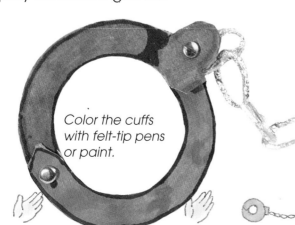

Color the cuffs with felt-tip pens or paint.

You need:

Strong cardboard, preferably corrugated
4 paper fasteners
4 pipe cleaners
Glue
Scissors
Silver foil
Felt-tip pens or paint

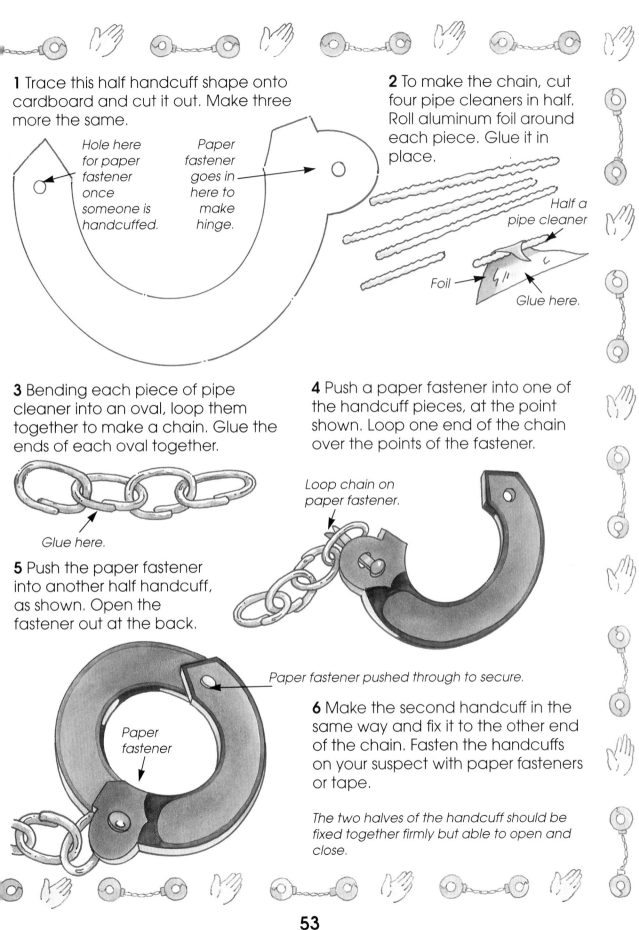

1 Trace this half handcuff shape onto cardboard and cut it out. Make three more the same.

Hole here for paper fastener once someone is handcuffed.

Paper fastener goes in here to make hinge.

2 To make the chain, cut four pipe cleaners in half. Roll aluminum foil around each piece. Glue it in place.

Half a pipe cleaner

Foil

Glue here.

3 Bending each piece of pipe cleaner into an oval, loop them together to make a chain. Glue the ends of each oval together.

Glue here.

4 Push a paper fastener into one of the handcuff pieces, at the point shown. Loop one end of the chain over the points of the fastener.

Loop chain on paper fastener.

5 Push the paper fastener into another half handcuff, as shown. Open the fastener out at the back.

Paper fastener pushed through to secure.

Paper fastener

6 Make the second handcuff in the same way and fix it to the other end of the chain. Fasten the handcuffs on your suspect with paper fasteners or tape.

The two halves of the handcuff should be fixed together firmly but able to open and close.

DETECTIVE FACTS

Here are some facts about police forces and detectives in the past.

Before there were proper police forces, **watchmen** guarded the streets at night. Every man over 16 took his turn to be watchman in his neighborhood. Settlers took the system to America and Australia. **Thief takers** were paid to catch criminals. Often they were criminals themselves and were hated by most people.

In 1829, Sir Robert Peel set up the **London Metropolitan Police Force**. Policemen were nicknamed peelers or bobbies, after their founder.

The first **US police force** was set up in Boston in 1838. It contained just six men.

In 1750, London became the first city to have an organized police force. They were called the **Bow Street Runners**.

The Pinkerton National Detective Agency was set up in 1850 in the USA. Early Pinkerton detectives trailed criminals such as the Wild Bunch, and Butch Cassidy and the Sundance Kid. The agency still exists today.

Forensic science

Forensic scientists help detectives by examining the clues found at the scene of a crime. They use scientific techniques to study fingerprints, footprints, clothing, bloodstains, hairs, fibers, specks of dust and dirt, documents letters and handwriting. The latest developments in forensic science involve studying cells from a person's body. Everyone has their own slightly different cell pattern. This is a very accurate way of identifying a criminal.

Storybook detectives

Millions of people enjoy reading detective stories. Here are some of the most famous fictional detectives.

Sherlock Holmes
Created by Sir Arthur Conan Doyle. There are 60 Holmes stories in all. The first, *A Study in Scarlet*, was published in 1887. 113a Baker Street in London - Holmes's fictional address - is now a tourist attraction.

Hercule Poirot and Miss Marple
Created by Agatha Christie. Poirot is a short, balding Belgian detective with a little moustache. Miss Marple is an elderly lady living in an English village.

Inspector Maigret
Created by Georges Simenon. This pipe-smoking Parisian detective first appeared in stories in 1931.

Philip Marlowe
Created in 1939 by Raymond Chandler. The cool, witty Marlowe is an American private eye.

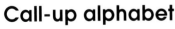

Call-up alphabet

Police sending radio messages use a special alphabet to spell out such things as names and car numbers. This makes sure the message gets through clearly and accurately. Use this alphabet to spell out your own message.

A Alpha	K Kilo	U Uncle
B Bravo	L Lima	V Victor
C Charlie	M Mike	W Whiskey
D Delta	N November	X X-ray
E Echo	O Oscar	Y Yankee
F Foxtrot	P Papa	Z Zulu
G Golf	Q Quebec	
H Hotel	R Romeo	
I India	S Sierra	
J Juliet	T Tango	

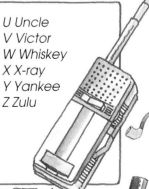

DETECTIVE WORDS

Alias A name which someone uses, perhaps to hide his or her real identity.

Alibi Proof that a person was somewhere other than at the scene of a crime when it was committed.

Burglary Breaking into a building to steal.

Charge Officially accuse a person of an offence.

Clue Something that helps solve a mystery.

Detective A person who tries to solve a crime, or carries out secret investigations. Some are plain-clothes members of a police force. Others are private detectives who are hired for a fee.

Evidence Information proving a fact.

Fraud Trickery or cheating.

HQ Headquarters, or main office of an organization.

Investigation An inquiry to try to discover who committed a crime.

Lead A helpful clue or piece of information.

Motive The reason a person has for committing a crime.

Offense A crime.

Robbery Theft using force.

Scene of the crime The place where a crime happened.

Statement A written, signed report by a suspect or a witness.

Surveillance Keeping a close watch on someone.

Suspect A person detectives think may have committed a crime.

Tail To follow someone.

Theft Stealing another person's property.

Witness A person who sees a crime being committed.

DID YOU KNOW?

• By 1988 Tommy Johns had been arrested 3000 times by detectives in Australia.

• In the 1st century AD the emperor Caesar Augustus formed the first police force in the city of Rome.

• Sir Arthur Conan Doyle, the creator of Sherlock Holmes, disliked the character so much that he eventually killed him off in one of his novels.

Part 3

CONTENTS

ABOUT THIS BOOK

In days of old no merchant ship could sail the oceans without risking capture by pirates! Treasure and the adventure of life on the open sea were the attractions of becoming a pirate. They were fierce fighters, plundering ships for their booty and taking prisoners for ransom.

This book has lots of ideas for making a pirate kit of your own. It shows you, step-by-step, how to make a pirate hat and eyepatch, weapons, telescope and your own treasure chest. You can also amaze friends by making a ship in a bottle.

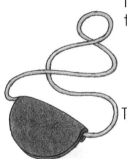

There are pirate games, too. Hunt for buried treasure with your friends, with the help of a handmade treasure map. Or play the fishing game and fish for sunken treasure on the ocean floor.

There are instructions for building a model of a real pirate ship and filling it with a crew. You can also learn how to tie useful knots and make your own pirate flag to terrorize your enemies.

Read some fascinating facts about the most feared real-life pirates and their adventures. You can find out who Calico Jack and Anne Bonny were and read about the other pirates who sailed with them. Learn, also, the special pirate words and sayings they used on board ship.

WHAT YOU NEED

On these pages you can see the things you need to become a pirate and to play all the games in the book.

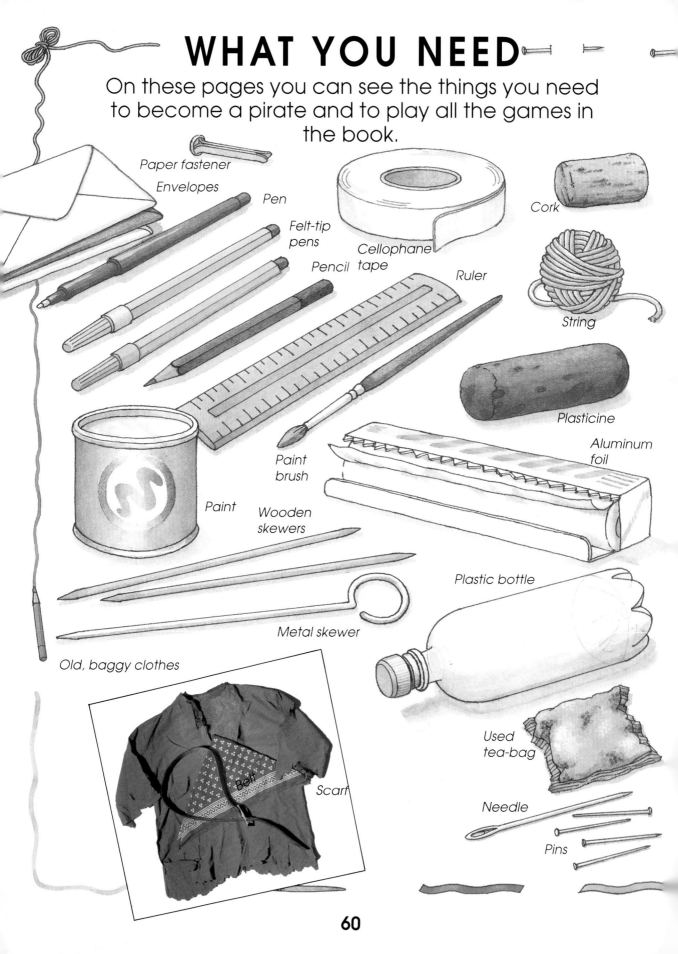

Paper fastener

Envelopes

Pen

Felt-tip pens

Cellophane tape

Cork

Pencil

Ruler

String

Paint brush

Plasticine

Aluminum foil

Paint

Wooden skewers

Plastic bottle

Metal skewer

Old, baggy clothes

Belt

Scarf

Used tea-bag

Needle

Pins

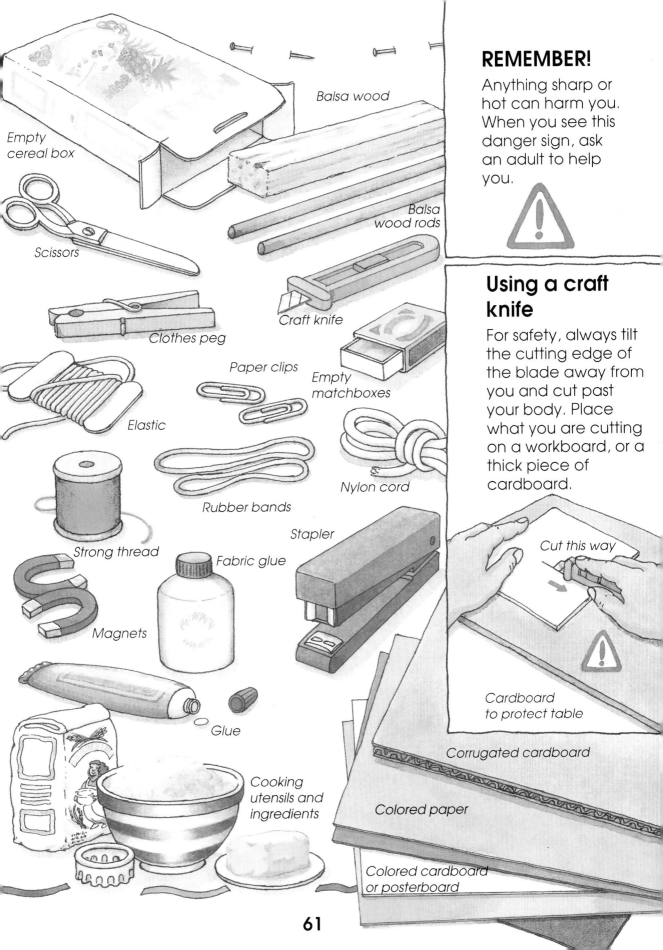

Empty
cereal box

Balsa wood

Scissors

Balsa
wood rods

Craft knife

Clothes peg

Paper clips

Empty
matchboxes

Elastic

Nylon cord

Rubber bands

Strong thread

Stapler

Fabric glue

Magnets

Glue

Cooking
utensils and
ingredients

REMEMBER!

Anything sharp or
hot can harm you.
When you see this
danger sign, ask
an adult to help
you.

Using a craft knife

For safety, always tilt
the cutting edge of
the blade away from
you and cut past
your body. Place
what you are cutting
on a workboard, or a
thick piece of
cardboard.

Cut this way

Cardboard
to protect table

Corrugated cardboard

Colored paper

Colored cardboard
or posterboard

61

PIRATE CLOTHES

Pirates wore loose, baggy clothes that were practical for climbing the rigging, or fighting. Here are some ideas for a pirate outfit of your own.

Make a beard out of black paper or material. Cut slits up from the bottom and tie around your ears with pieces of string.

Make a pirate hat or tie a scarf around your head.

Make an eyepatch.

Draw on scars with face paints.

Sew hoop earrings onto a scarf. Pirates believed that wearing earrings improved their eyesight!

Wear a big, baggy shirt or t-shirt, loose trousers, a wide belt or scarf around your waist.

Make a cutlass or pistol (see p. 64-65)

Torn and patched clothes look good (ask an adult's permission before tearing clothes!)

You could think up a fierce piratical name too. How about One-eyed Jack, or Cutlass Kate?

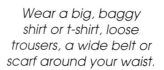

Pirate hat and eyepatch

You need:

Black paper
White paper or paint
Gold or silver paper or paint
String or elastic
Glue, stapler
Pencil, ruler, scissors

1 Fold a sheet of black paper (11³/₄in x 11³/₄in) in half. Draw a hat shape and cut it out.

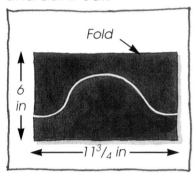

Fold

6 in

11³/₄ in

2 Paint a skull and crossbones on the front, or cut them out of paper and glue on.

Decorate the edges with gold or silver paper.

3 Staple the front and back together at the sides, to fit your head.

Staple here

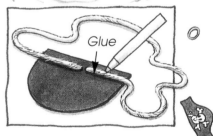

Eyepatch

1 Cut a half circle out of black paper.

2 Cut a piece of elastic or string long enough to tie around your head. Glue it to the straight edge of the paper.

Glue

3 Fold the edge over and glue again.

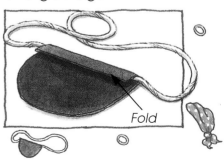

Fold

ARMS

All pirates carried weapons - called arms -
for attacking their enemies and robbing
merchant ships. Here are two fierce-looking
weapons to make.

Cutlass

A cutlass was a short sword with a
curved blade for slicing at the enemy.

You need:

Corrugated cardboard, 23$\frac{1}{2}$ in x 8in
Silver or gold posterboard, foil or paint
Craft knife
Pen
Glue

1 Draw the shape of the
cutlass on thick
cardboard and use a
craft knife to cut it out.
Trace around it and cut
out another identical
shape. Glue the shapes
together.

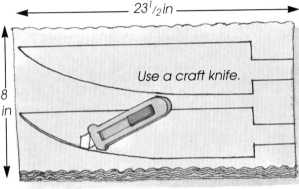

← 23$\frac{1}{2}$in →

8 in

Use a craft knife.

2 Trace around the cutlass on
silver or gold-colored posterboard.
Turn it over and trace around it
again. Cut out the shapes and
glue them either side of the
cutlass.

*You could use silver foil or paint
instead of posterboard.*

3 Cut out the guard from silver or
gold posterboard. Measure the width
of the cutlass handle and draw and
cut out slots in the guard the same
width for it to fit through.

← 13in →

3 in

1$\frac{1}{2}$in   1$\frac{1}{2}$in

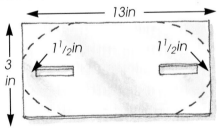

4 Slide the guard on to
the handle and glue it on.

*Cut a small notch here
to fix the guard firmly.*

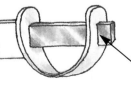

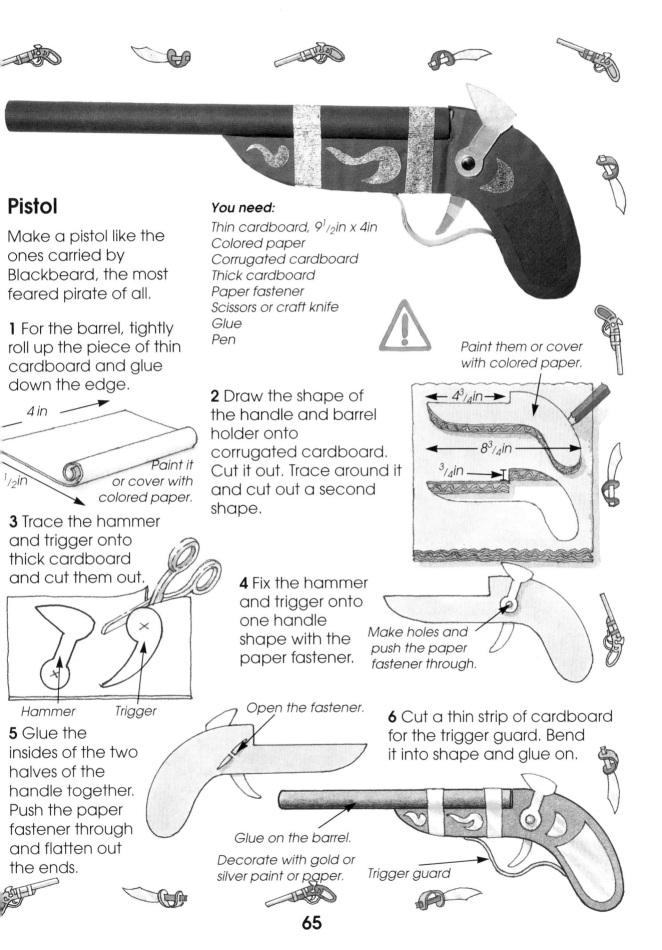

Pistol

Make a pistol like the ones carried by Blackbeard, the most feared pirate of all.

You need:

Thin cardboard, $9^1/_2$in x 4in
Colored paper
Corrugated cardboard
Thick cardboard
Paper fastener
Scissors or craft knife
Glue
Pen

1 For the barrel, tightly roll up the piece of thin cardboard and glue down the edge.

4 in

$^1/_2$in

Paint it or cover with colored paper.

2 Draw the shape of the handle and barrel holder onto corrugated cardboard. Cut it out. Trace around it and cut out a second shape.

Paint them or cover with colored paper.

$4^3/_4$in

$8^3/_4$in

$^3/_4$in

3 Trace the hammer and trigger onto thick cardboard and cut them out.

Hammer   *Trigger*

4 Fix the hammer and trigger onto one handle shape with the paper fastener.

Make holes and push the paper fastener through.

5 Glue the insides of the two halves of the handle together. Push the paper fastener through and flatten out the ends.

Open the fastener.

6 Cut a thin strip of cardboard for the trigger guard. Bend it into shape and glue on.

Glue on the barrel.

Decorate with gold or silver paint or paper.

Trigger guard

PIRATE SHIP

The best pirate ships were small, fast and easy to steer for a surprise attack and quick getaway. If a pirate crew captured a better ship, they kept it!

Ask an adult to help you make this model ship and crew.

You need:

Small empty cereal box
$^3/_4$in balsa rods
$^1/_4$in balsa rods
Cardboard or Posterboard
Colored paper
String or thread
Glue, scissors

1 For the **hull**, cut two cardboard strips, 14in long and deeper than the side of the box. Bend them into shape and glue them to the cereal box.

Fold cardboard at front for bow.

Box

Curve cardboard around for stern.

Jib sail

Forestay

Foremast

2 To make the **deck**, trace around the hull on paper and cut out the shape just inside the line. Rule on lines for planks and glue the deck down on the box.

Rule lines

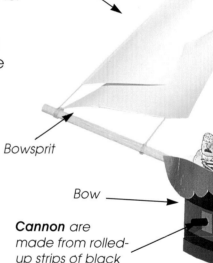

Bowsprit

Bow

Hull

3 For **masts**, make three holes through the deck into the box. Cut two $^3/_4$in balsa rods 15$^3/_4$in long and one 19in long. Glue them into the deck.

Cannon are made from rolled-up strips of black paper glued into holes.

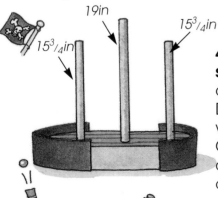

19in

15$^3/_4$in

15$^3/_4$in

4 Draw 3 sets of **shrouds** (rigging) on grey paper. Draw on the lines with black pen. Cut out and make a hole in the center of each.

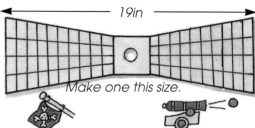

13in

1$^1/_2$ in

Make two this size.

19in

2 in

Make one this size.

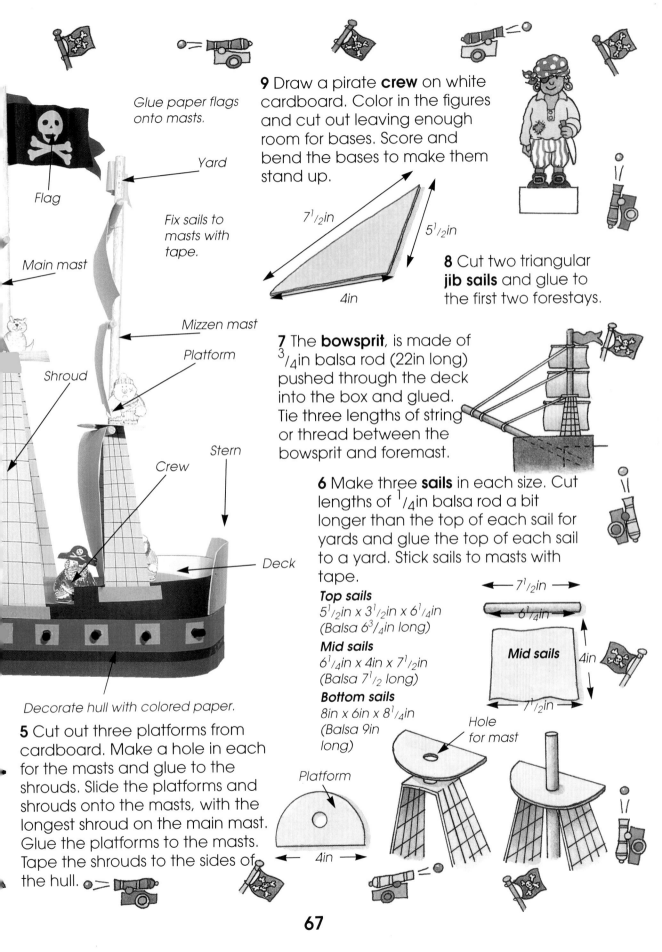

Glue paper flags onto masts.

Flag

Yard

Fix sails to masts with tape.

Main mast

Mizzen mast

Platform

Shroud

Crew

Stern

Deck

Decorate hull with colored paper.

9 Draw a pirate **crew** on white cardboard. Color in the figures and cut out leaving enough room for bases. Score and bend the bases to make them stand up.

$7^1/_2$in

$5^1/_2$in

4in

8 Cut two triangular **jib sails** and glue to the first two forestays.

7 The **bowsprit**, is made of $^3/_4$in balsa rod (22in long) pushed through the deck into the box and glued. Tie three lengths of string or thread between the bowsprit and foremast.

6 Make three **sails** in each size. Cut lengths of $^1/_4$in balsa rod a bit longer than the top of each sail for yards and glue the top of each sail to a yard. Stick sails to masts with tape.

Top sails
$5^1/_2$in x $3^1/_2$in x $6^1/_4$in
(Balsa $6^3/_4$in long)

Mid sails
$6^1/_4$in x 4in x $7^1/_2$in
(Balsa $7^1/_2$ long)

Bottom sails
8in x 6in x $8^1/_4$in
(Balsa 9in long)

$7^1/_2$in

$6^1/_4$in

Mid sails

4in

$7^1/_2$in

5 Cut out three platforms from cardboard. Make a hole in each for the masts and glue to the shrouds. Slide the platforms and shrouds onto the masts, with the longest shroud on the main mast. Glue the platforms to the masts. Tape the shrouds to the sides of the hull.

Platform

Hole for mast

4in

PIRATE TREASURE

Most pirates robbed merchant ships carrying silks, spices and tobacco, and sold the cargo at the next port. But sometimes they were lucky and found treasure - gold coins and precious jewels - on board.

Treasure chest

Make this pirate's treasure chest with jewels and coins to fill it - or keep your own special treasures inside.

You need:

Thin cardboard or
  posterboard
Colored paper
Aluminum foil and
colored foil
Candy wrappers
Cellophane tape, glue
Pencil, ruler
Scissors

1 Draw this shape onto cardboard. Score and bend along the dotted lines.

Score

6¹/₄in

5¹/₂in

Flap

2 Glue the flaps to the inside of the chest's sides.

Glue flaps down

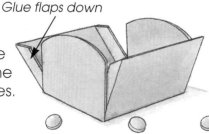

3 Cut out the lid. Bend it slightly to make it curve. Fix it to the chest with tape hinges.

3in

2³/₄in

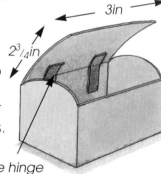

Tape hinge

4 Cut thin strips of colored paper for bands. Cut out a lock and handles. Glue them onto the chest.

5 Make jewels and coins from aluminum foil and candy wrappers.

You could line your treasure chest with tissue paper or material first.

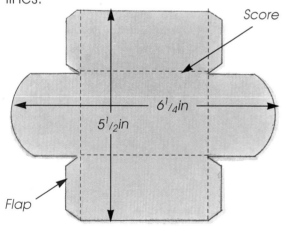

Treasure hunt

Make a map of your house or garden and use it to play a game of pirates' treasure hunt with your friends.

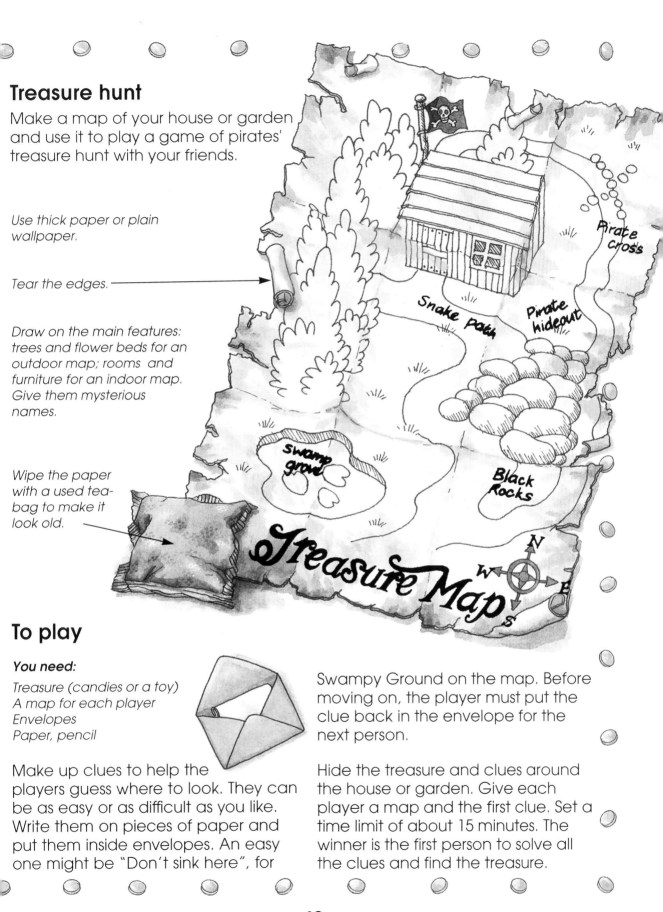

Use thick paper or plain wallpaper.

Tear the edges. ──────→

Draw on the main features: trees and flower beds for an outdoor map; rooms and furniture for an indoor map. Give them mysterious names.

Wipe the paper with a used tea-bag to make it look old.

To play

You need:

Treasure (candies or a toy)
A map for each player
Envelopes
Paper, pencil

Make up clues to help the players guess where to look. They can be as easy or as difficult as you like. Write them on pieces of paper and put them inside envelopes. An easy one might be "Don't sink here", for

Swampy Ground on the map. Before moving on, the player must put the clue back in the envelope for the next person.

Hide the treasure and clues around the house or garden. Give each player a map and the first clue. Set a time limit of about 15 minutes. The winner is the first person to solve all the clues and find the treasure.

LIFE AT SEA

Many pirates went to sea to escape the hardships of life on land. But life at sea could be even tougher.

Ship's biscuits

Mix your own "pirate potion" - orange juice, grape juice and lemonade.

At sea, fresh food and water quickly ran out. Pirates ate mainly salted meat and hard "ship's biscuits," which had weevils - tiny beetles - wriggling about in them!

Make your own "ship's biscuits." These taste much better than the real ones!

You need:

$1^3/_4$ cups self-raising flour
4 tbsp soft brown sugar
4 tbsp soft margarine
1 teaspoon cinnamon
1 tablespoon corn syrup
Chocolate chips
Pasty cutter

ASK AN ADULT TO LIGHT THE OVEN

1 Set the oven at 350°F. Sift flour into a large mixing bowl. Stir in sugar and cinnamon.

2 Rub in margarine with your fingertips until the mixture looks like fine breadcrumbs.

3 Stir in syrup. Make the mixture into a dough with your fingers.

$^1/_4$in thick

4 Roll out the dough to about $^3/_4$in thick. Cut out shapes with pastry cutter.

5 Press in chocolate chips (for weevils). Place shapes onto a greased oven tray.

6 Cook for 10-15 minutes, or until golden brown, on the center shelf of the oven. Cool on a wire tray.

Porthole picture

It was exciting when another ship, new land or a strange sea animal came into sight. Here is a porthole picture to make and hang on your wall.

You need:

Colored paper
Gold or silver cardboard
or posterboard, felt-tip pens
Glue, cellophane tape

1 Cut out two large paper circles, one light blue and the other dark blue (you could draw around a plate). Cut the dark circle in half. Then cut off a wavy strip and glue the rest onto the light circle.

Cut off a 1¹⁄₄in strip making a wavy line.

2 Decide on your scene. Draw and cut it out of colored paper. Keep the shapes very simple. Here are some ideas:

3 Arrange the shapes on the background before gluing them on. Draw on details with felt-tips.

4 For the frame, draw a circle the same size as before, on gold or silver cardboard. Draw a smaller circle inside (draw around a smaller plate) Cut out the frame and glue it on.

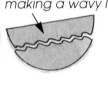

Whale

Desert Island

Ships

Leave a few inches clear around the edge for frame.

Glue on cardboard for bolts or draw them.
Tape a piece of string to the back so you can hang up your picture.

INTO BATTLE!

When the lookout spotted a merchant ship on the horizon, the pirates hoisted the Jolly Roger flag and got ready to attack!

Catapult

Make this catapult and use it to play an exciting sea-battle game.

You need:

Block of balsa wood, $5^1/_2$in x 2in x $^1/_2$in
$1^1/_4$in length of wooden skewer
Long elastic band, clothes peg
Thin cardboard, or posterboard
Craft knife
Metal skewer

ASK AN ADULT TO HELP YOU

Fit peg over skewer.

Use a craft knife.

$^1/_2$in

2in

$5^1/_2$in

Wooden skewer

$1^1/_4$in

Make hole with a metal skewer.

1 Cut two notches, about $^1/_2$in deep, into one end of the balsa block.

2 Make a hole about $1^1/_4$in from the other end. Glue in the piece of wooden skewer.

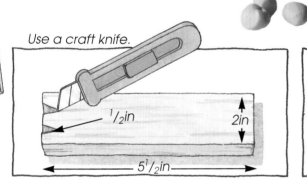

3in

Elastic band doubled over.

$^3/_4$ in

3 Cut out the sling from thin cardboard. Make two holes and thread the elastic band through.

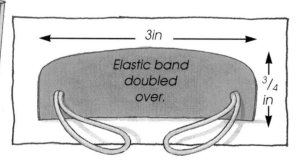

4 Glue or tape the ends of the elastic band around the notches.

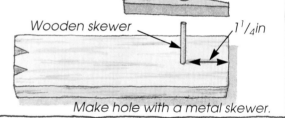

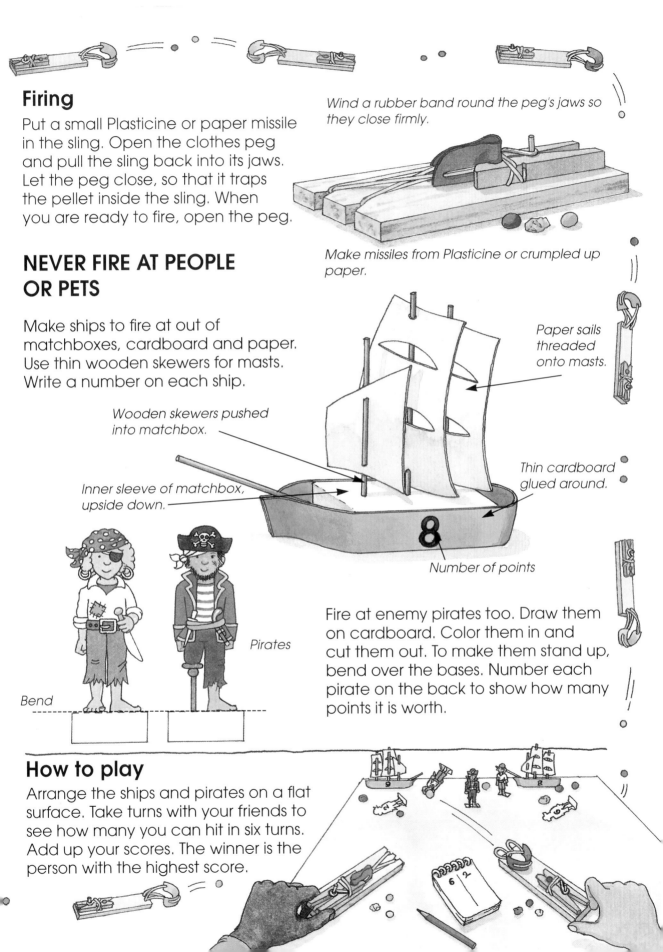

Firing

Put a small Plasticine or paper missile in the sling. Open the clothes peg and pull the sling back into its jaws. Let the peg close, so that it traps the pellet inside the sling. When you are ready to fire, open the peg.

NEVER FIRE AT PEOPLE OR PETS

Make ships to fire at out of matchboxes, cardboard and paper. Use thin wooden skewers for masts. Write a number on each ship.

Wind a rubber band round the peg's jaws so they close firmly.

Make missiles from Plasticine or crumpled up paper.

Paper sails threaded onto masts.

Wooden skewers pushed into matchbox.

Inner sleeve of matchbox, upside down.

Thin cardboard glued around.

8

Number of points

Pirates

Bend

Fire at enemy pirates too. Draw them on cardboard. Color them in and cut them out. To make them stand up, bend over the bases. Number each pirate on the back to show how many points it is worth.

How to play

Arrange the ships and pirates on a flat surface. Take turns with your friends to see how many you can hit in six turns. Add up your scores. The winner is the person with the highest score.

PIRATE PASTIMES

In their spare time pirates mended their clothes, danced and sang, or played games. They played "bones", a game with dice, and checkers.

Ship in a bottle

Pirates who had been craftsmen on land enjoyed carving and making things.

Ship

1 Carefully cut off the end of the bottle with a craft knife. Save the cut-off piece.

Cut about 1¹/₄in from the end.

2 On the balsa block, draw the bow and stern shapes. Carefully carve the shape of the hull.

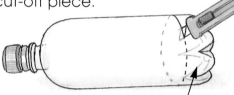

Bow *Stern* *Hull*

3 Cut thin wooden skewers to length for the masts and bowsprit. Make holes in the deck with a metal skewer. Glue in the masts.

Bowsprit *Masts*

You need:

Empty 0.5 liter plastic soda bottle
Balsa wood block, about 3in x ³/₄in x ³/₄in
2 thin wooden skewers
Thin cardboard or posterboard
Craft knife, metal skewer
Felt-tip pens, cotton thread
Glue, cellophane tape, Plasticine
Pencil, ruler

4 Draw and cut out sails from thin cardboard. Copy these shapes. Make a hole in the top and bottom of the three main sails as shown. Thread the sails on to the masts and glue.

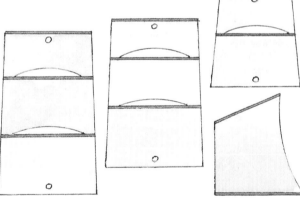

Foremast

5 Cut out three triangular jibsails. Knot three cotton threads between the bowsprit and the foremast. Glue on the jibsails.

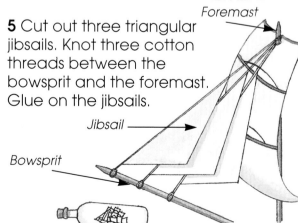

Jibsail

Bowsprit

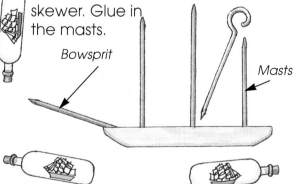

74

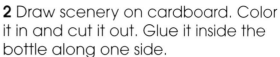

Inside the bottle

1 Squash flat some blue Plasticine for the sea. Glue it inside the bottle.

2 Draw scenery on cardboard. Color it in and cut it out. Glue it inside the bottle along one side.

3 Glue the ship inside the bottle, pressing it down firmly into the Plasticine.

4 Stick back the cut section of bottle with clear tape. If you do it carefully, no one will know how you got the ship in the bottle!

LOOKOUT

Pirate lookouts kept watch from the crow's nest, high up on the main mast. They scanned the horizon through a telescope, looking for ships to rob or dangerous rocks.

Telescope

You need:

Thin white cardboard or
 posterboard
Black paper or paint
Gold paper or paint
Scissors
Glue
Ruler
Pencil

1 Measure and cut out three pieces of cardboard.

$6^3/_4$in
$6^3/_4$in

$5^1/_2$in
$6^3/_4$in

$4^3/_4$in
$6^3/_4$in

2 Roll up each piece into a long tube and glue it along the edge.

Paint the tubes, or cover them with black paper.

3 Cut a long strip of cardboard and glue it around one end of the middle tube.

Wind it around and around.

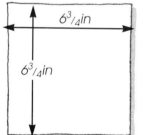

2in

$15^3/_4$in

4 Cut another cardboard strip and glue it around one end of the thinnest tube.

Make sure the tubes fit inside each other snugly.

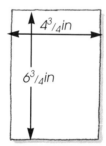

2in

$9^3/_4$in

Fattest tube   Middle tube   Thinnest tube

5 Glue thin strips of gold cardboard or paper around the ends of the tubes for decoration.

6 Push the middle tube inside the fattest tube and the thinnest into the middle tube.

Glue strips at both ends.

Glue strips around this end only.

Compass

To find their way about the oceans, pirates had to know how to navigate. They had sea-maps, called charts, and instruments, such as the compass, to help them.

The needle inside a compass is magnetic. However it is held, it always turns towards Earth's magnetic North Pole.

Try this experiment with a floating cork and needle. You will need a pocket compass to check the result.

Needle magnetized by stroking it 20 times in the same direction with a magnet.

Stick needle on cork with tape or poster-tack.

The needle should always turn towards north.

$^1/_4$in section of cork

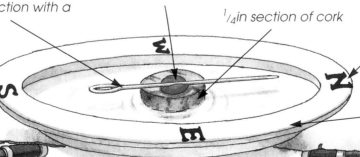

W

S

N

E

Shallow dish of water with a drop of detergent added.

DAVY JONES'S LOCKER

Nearly all pirates believed in sea monsters, and mythical creatures such as mermaids. Davy Jones was the main spirit of the sea, and pirates called the ocean floor "Davy Jones's locker."

Make this game and fish for sunken treasure in Davy Jones's locker. Beware - you might hook some sea monsters, too!

You need:

2 pieces of colored cardboard
 or posterboard, $23^1/_2$in x $9^3/_4$in
Thin cardboard, colored paper
Felt-tip markers
2 or 3 sticks (balsa rods or short garden canes)
2 or 3 strong magnets, metal paper clips
Strong thread, glue, scissors, tape

1 On each piece of cardboard measure half way across and draw a line down. Then measure 2in in from one edge, and draw another line down.

2 Score and bend along the lines you have drawn.

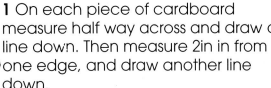
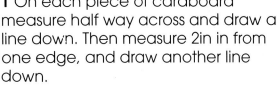

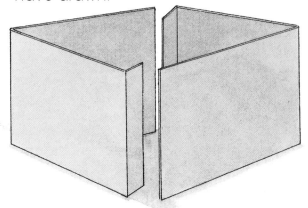

3 Turn the pieces of cardboard over. Draw on an undersea scene with felt-tips, or glue on shapes cut out from colored paper.

4 Stand the cardboard pieces upright. Glue them together along the tabs.

Glue tabs inside.

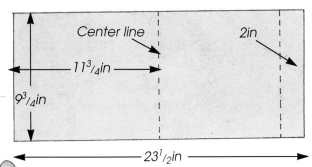

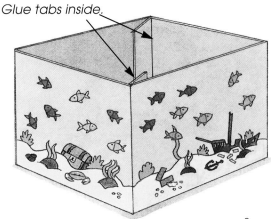

78

Things to catch

On thin cardboard, draw the outlines of fish and other things to catch, such as sea monsters, crabs, octopuses, anchors, old boots and treasure chests. Cut them out. Decide on a score for each object, such as 10 for a treasure chest, 5 for an octopus and 1 for a boot.

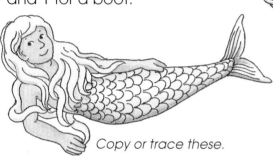

Copy or trace these.

Fix a paper clip to each object.

Fishing rods

Wind and tie a long piece of thread to one end of each stick. Secure with tape. Tie a strong magnet onto the other end.

Write a number on the back.

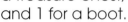
Wind the thread around.

How to play

Two or three people can play. Put the objects inside the box. At the word "Go," the players have two minutes to fish out as many objects as they can. When time is up, the players add up their scores. The winner is the person with the highest score.

JOLLY ROGER

To fool the enemy, pirates would sometimes fly an ordinary flag and then at the last moment hoist the Jolly Roger and attack.

Make this fearsome flag and terrify your enemies. Follow this design or, like real pirate captains, make up your own.

Calico Jack's flag

Blackbeard's flag

You need:

Black fabric, $15^3/_4$in x $11^3/_4$in
White or colored fabric or paper
Fabric glue
Scissors
Pins
Stick for flagpole

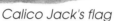

1 Fold a piece of paper in half. Draw half a skull on the fold and one bone. Cut them out and you will have a whole skull and two bones.

Fold

Pins

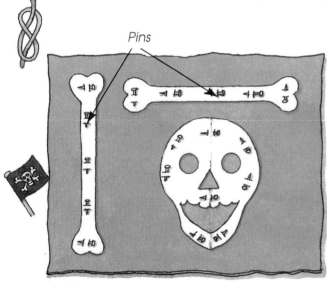

2 If you are using material, pin the shapes onto it and cut around them.

Fold over and glue this edge.

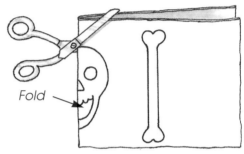

3 Glue the paper or material shapes onto the flag. Glue or tape a stick down the left-hand side.

KNOTS

Pirates needed to know how to tie all kinds of knots for securing sails and ropes and for tying up prisoners.

Learn to tie these useful knots. For each knot you need about $35\frac{1}{4}$in of nylon cord, about $\frac{1}{4}$in thick.

Figure of eight
Stops the end of a rope from coming undone.

❶  **❷**  **❸** *Pull*   *Pull*

Clove hitch
For tying things together or fastening.

❶ 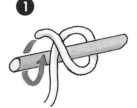 **❷** 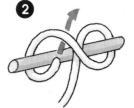 **❸** *Pull* 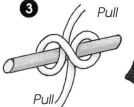 *Pull*

Bowline
Makes a strong loop that will not slip.

❶ 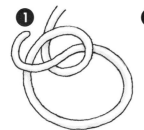 **❷** 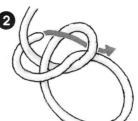 **❸** *Pull* *Pull*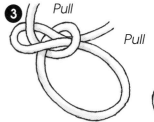

Sheepshank
Useful for shortening a long rope.

❶ 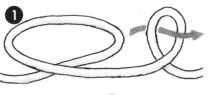 **❷**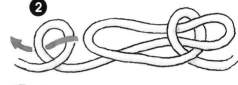

❸ *Pull* *Pull*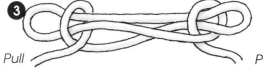

Round turn and two-half-hitches
Use to tie a boat to its mooring.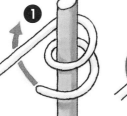

❶ 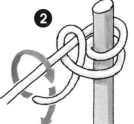 **❷**  **❸** *Pull*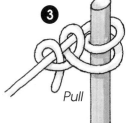

PIRATE FACTS

Pirates, or sea-robbers, have plundered the seas since the earliest times. There are still pirates today, robbing ships in the South China Sea.

The Golden Age

The most notorious pirates lived during the 16th, 17th and 18th centuries. This time became known as the Golden Age of Piracy.

The discovery of America and the growth in trade between continents meant there were more ships carrying precious cargoes across the oceans for pirates to plunder.

Many men became pirates to find adventure and freedom. Some were runaway criminals, and others were recruited from captured ships. Pirates were all nationalities. The Japanese and Chinese were especially fierce and cruel.

The best place for plunder was the Caribbean Sea. It was on the route home for ships carrying gold from South America to Europe, and it was full of tiny islands for pirates to hide in.

A hundred lashes with the cat o' nine tails - a stick with nine knotted ropes attached.

Pirate punishments

New crew members had to sign a set of rules, called "articles," when they joined a ship. Any pirate who caused trouble, or disobeyed the ship's articles, was given one of these severe punishments:

Stuffing the offender's mouth with oakum (strands of rope soaked in tar) and then setting it alight.

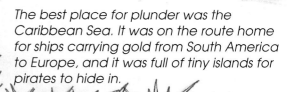

Keelhauled - tied to a rope and dropped into the sea, then hauled underneath the boat, scraping against the clusters of barnacles.

Marooned on a desert island with only a gun and some water.

Famous pirates

Long Ben *(real name John Avery)* was a pirate in the 17th century. He once captured a treasure ship carrying an Indian Mogul Emperor's daughter and sailed it to the pirate island of Madagascar. He lived there as a king, but ended his life in England in poverty.

Blackbeard *(real name Edward Teach)* was a buccaneer and the most feared pirate of all. To terrify his enemies, he would go into battle armed with six pistols and with slow-burning fuses tucked under his hat.

Captain Bartholomew Roberts robbed more than 400 ships between 1719 and 1722. He liked to wear fine clothes, especially in battle. He was religious, drank only tea, and insisted his crew were in bed by 8pm.

Calico Jack *(real name John Rackham)* wore costumes of colorful cotton. He plundered ships in the Caribbean between 1718 and 1720 until he was caught and hanged.

Women pirates

Women were usually forbidden on board pirate ships, but some female pirates did exist.

Anne Bonny fell in love with the pirate captain, Calico Jack, and ran away to sea with him disguised as a man. She was a fierce fighter and one of the best pirates on the ship.

Mary Read was brought up as a boy. She was a footman, soldier and sailor before becoming a pirate. She joined the same crew as Anne Bonny and both were captured in 1720. They were sentenced to hang but then allowed to live as they were both pregnant.

PIRATE WORDS

Arms Weapons.

Articles Rules that pirates had to obey while on board ship.

Barnacles Tiny, hard-shelled sea creatures that cling to a ship's hull.

Black Jack A pirate flag.

Booty Stolen goods.

Buccaneer Outlaw turned pirate.

Cargo Goods carried by a ship.

Cat o' nine tails A whip with nine knotted ropes attached, used for punishing sailors.

Compass An instrument for finding direction.

Crow's nest A lookout platform high up on a ship's mast.

Cutlass A curved, one-edged sword used by sailors.

Davy Jones's locker Sailor's name for the ocean floor.

Galley A ship's kitchen, or a ship which had oars as well as sails.

Jolly Roger A pirate flag.

Keelhaul To drag a person by a rope under a ship from one side to the other.

Lookout Someone who keeps watch against danger.

Loot Stolen goods; plunder.

Marooned Abandoned on a desert island.

Merchant ship A trading ship.

Navigate To plot the route.

Oakum Strands of tarred rope which were stuffed between planks to stop a ship from leaking.

Pieces of eight Spanish silver coins stamped with a figure eight.

Plunder Stolen goods.

Privateer A person authorized to attack enemy ships.

Prize A captured ship; booty.

Ransom Money or goods paid for the release of a hostage.

Weevil A type of beetle.

Yellow Jack A flag pirates flew when they had disease on board ship.

Pirate sayings:

"Belay that noise" - *"Be quiet!"*

"Avast" - *"Stop!"*

"Shiver me timbers" - *"Goodness me!"*

"Ahoy there" - *"Hey!"*

"Tell it to the parrot" - *"Tell everyone."*

"Surrender ye swabs!" - *"Give in you creeps!"*

"Scupper that ship" - *"Sink that ship by blowing holes in it."*

"Land ahoy" - *"There's land in sight."*

"This grog tastes like bilge water!" - *"This drink tastes horrible!"*

DID YOU KNOW?

• Not all pirates were outlaws. Sir Francis Drake was knighted by Queen Elizabeth I because he robbed Spanish treasure ships for her.

• Captain William Kidd became a pirate-hunter and then turned to piracy himself. He was hanged at Execution Dock in London, England in 1701.

• Real pirates never forced their prisoners to walk the plank! This was invented by storytellers.

Part 4

Explorers

CONTENTS

ABOUT THIS BOOK

Explorers travel into unknown territory, through dense forests and jungles, across scorching, dry deserts or frozen polar wastelands. Some dive far beneath the sea and others are rocketed into outer space. Explorers are brave and love adventure.

This book has lots of fun ideas for playing explorers. It shows you, step-by-step, how to make a mosquito hat to wear in the jungle, a survival-kit carrier to take with you on any expedition, and ideas for simple shelters to build.

Bring the jungle into your own bedroom by making a giant picture on the wall, or be a wildlife explorer and collect specimens in a handmade bug jar. Make alien masks and your own astronaut helmet and oxygen pack for a space adventure.

There are exploring games, too. Play Arctic racing with your friends, or help explorers escape from a pyramid maze.

There are also fascinating facts about some famous real-life explorers. You can learn useful survival tips and distress signals and brush up on the terms explorers use on expeditions.

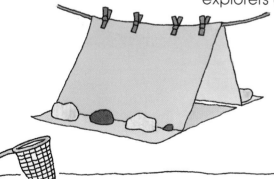

WHAT YOU NEED

On these pages you can see the things you need to play the games in the book, and to make your own kits for all kinds of expeditions.

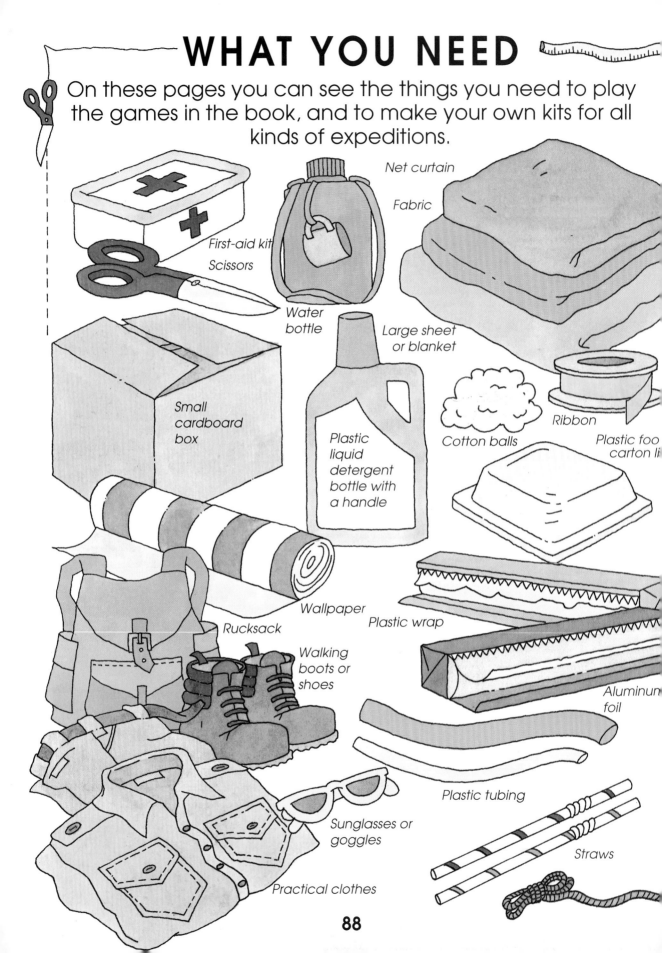

Net curtain

Fabric

First-aid kit

Scissors

Water bottle

Large sheet or blanket

Ribbon

Small cardboard box

Plastic liquid detergent bottle with a handle

Cotton balls

Plastic foo carton li

Wallpaper

Plastic wrap

Rucksack

Walking boots or shoes

Aluminun foil

Plastic tubing

Sunglasses or goggles

Straws

Practical clothes

Rations

Ruler

Paint brush

Pencil

Felt-tip pens

Pen top

Plasticine

Cellophane tape

Rubber bands

Craft knife

String

Small glass jar with a plastic lid

Large glass jar

Poster-tack

Paints

Colored paper

Colored cardboard or posterboard

Plastic bottles

Fabric glue

Glue

Using a craft knife

For safety, always tilt the cutting edge of the blade away from you and cut past your body. Place what you are cutting on a workboard, or a thick piece of cardboard.

Cut this way

Cardboard to protect table

REMEMBER!

Anything sharp or hot can harm you. When you see this danger sign, ask an adult to help you.

CLOTHES

Explorers wear comfortable, practical clothes that suit the climate and kind of terrain they are travelling in. Here are some ideas to help you make your own explorer outfits.

In a cold climate you need: In a hot climate you need:

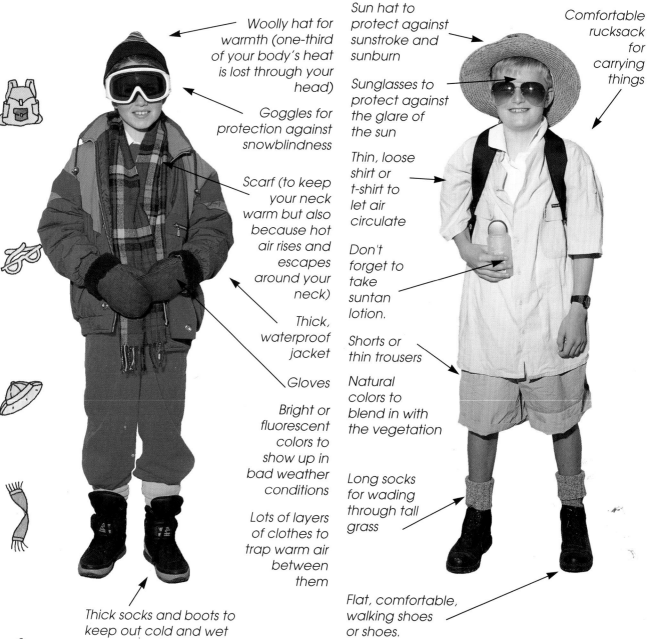

Woolly hat for warmth (one-third of your body's heat is lost through your head)

Goggles for protection against snowblindness

Scarf (to keep your neck warm but also because hot air rises and escapes around your neck)

Thick, waterproof jacket

Gloves

Bright or fluorescent colors to show up in bad weather conditions

Lots of layers of clothes to trap warm air between them

Thick socks and boots to keep out cold and wet

Sun hat to protect against sunstroke and sunburn

Sunglasses to protect against the glare of the sun

Thin, loose shirt or t-shirt to let air circulate

Don't forget to take suntan lotion.

Shorts or thin trousers

Natural colors to blend in with the vegetation

Long socks for wading through tall grass

Flat, comfortable, walking shoes or shoes.

Comfortable rucksack for carrying things

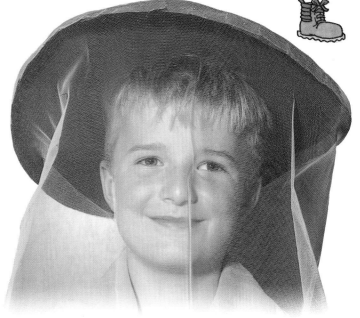

Anti-mosquito hat

Make this anti-mosquito hat for protection against flying pests in tropical climates.

You need:

Large piece of cardboard
Piece of thin net curtain
Piece of string
Fabric glue
Scissors
Cellophane tape

You could use the netting from fruit or vegetable bags instead of net curtain.

1 Draw around a large plate or tray onto the cardboard and cut the circle out. Cut $^3/_4$ in slits all around the edge.

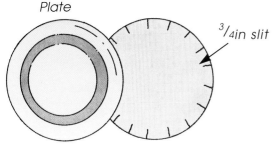

Plate

$^3/_4$in slit

2 Measure around your head with a piece of string and tie a knot. Tape the string to the cardboard and cut out the circle inside it.

Cut out a circle to fit your head.

You could attach the netting to an old hat with a brim.

3 Remove the string and place the ring on your head. Close the net curtain around to see how much you need.

The net curtain should reach down to your shoulders.

4 Bend down the slits on the brim and glue the net curtain to them.

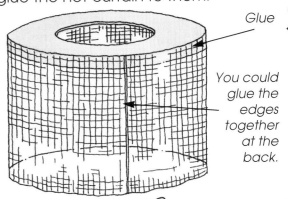

Glue

You could glue the edges together at the back.

SURVIVAL

People cannot survive without food and water.
Explorers must carry a supply of food and plenty
of water to keep healthy.

Fresh food quickly goes off, so real
explorers take dried, powdered and
canned foods that give them a
balanced diet of proteins, fats and
carbohydrates.

Here are some suggestions for
energy-giving rations that you could
take with you:

Nuts

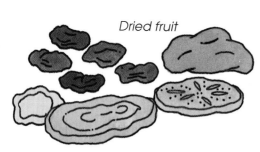

Dried fruit

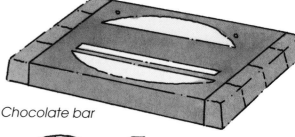

Chocolate bar

Fresh water
in a clean,
plastic
bottle

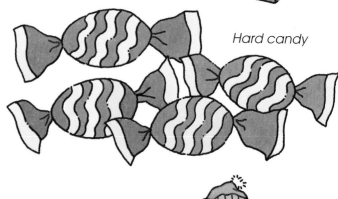

Hard candy

Water is very important.
Without it, you would
die in a few days. When
real explorers run out of
water they drink melted
snow or ice, dew or
rainwater.

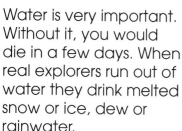

Survival-kit carrier

Make this handy survival-kit carrier. Pack it with items you need for your expedition.

You need:

Two pieces of thick fabric
 (12^1/$_2$in x 8^3/$_4$ in, and 12^1/$_2$in x 4in)
Fabric glue
Tape or ribbon (17^3/$_4$in long)
Scissors
Ruler
Survival equipment, including first-aid
 items (band-aids, bandages, scissors,
 tweezers, insect-bite cream, snake-bite
 lotion), and string, compass, penknife etc.

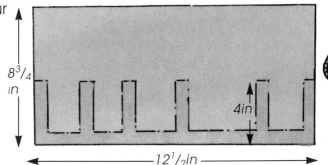

8^3/$_4$ in

4in

12^1/$_2$in

1 Spread fabric glue along the bottom and sides and in lines as shown. Make as many spaces as you need for all your items.

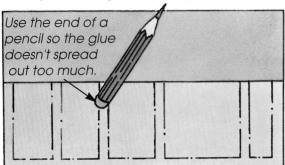

Use the end of a pencil so the glue doesn't spread out too much.

2 Glue on the smaller fabric strip (it looks good in a different color). Press down firmly along the lines with the end of a pencil. Leave to dry. Then store your equipment in the pockets.

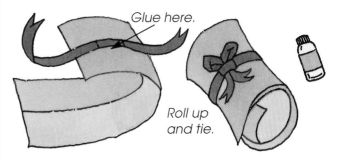

Glue here.

Roll up and tie.

3 Glue the middle of your tape or ribbon on the back of one edge. Roll up the kit from the other end. Wrap the tape or ribbon around the bundle and tie a bow so it can be quickly undone in an emergency.

Fill a small empty bottle with water and pretend it is "snake-bite" lotion!

FINDING THE WAY

Explorers need maps to guide them through unfamiliar territory, and to point out danger areas such as swampy ground, or obstacles such as high mountains.

The first people to explore a new territory make a map of the area giving a route for future travellers to follow.

Make this imaginary explorer's map and use it to play a game with your friends.

You need:

Large sheet of paper (19in x 14in)
Colored paper
Felt-tip pens
Scissors, poster-tack
Pencil, ruler

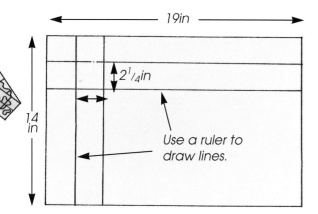

Use a ruler to draw lines.

1 Make a pencil mark every 6cm along all four sides of the sheet of paper. Join each mark with the one opposite to divide the paper into squares.

2 Number the squares down the left-hand side 1 to 6. Write the letters A to H in the squares across the top.

Map features

Trace two of each of the features on page 95 onto colored paper. Cut them out and stick poster-tack on the back. Each feature is worth the number of points shown.

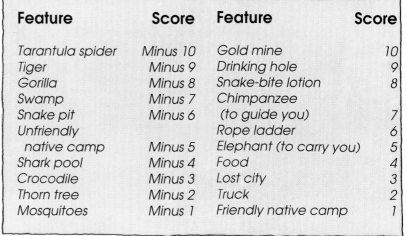

Feature	Score	Feature	Score
Tarantula spider	Minus 10	Gold mine	10
Tiger	Minus 9	Drinking hole	9
Gorilla	Minus 8	Snake-bite lotion	8
Swamp	Minus 7	Chimpanzee (to guide you)	7
Snake pit	Minus 6		
Unfriendly native camp	Minus 5	Rope ladder	6
		Elephant (to carry you)	5
Shark pool	Minus 4	Food	4
Crocodile	Minus 3	Lost city	3
Thorn tree	Minus 2	Truck	2
Mosquitoes	Minus 1	Friendly native camp	1

How to play

One player takes the map and, without the other players seeing, sticks each feature in a square, using the blob of poster-tack. The blank squares which are left are not worth any points.

Each of the other players then takes turns naming a square on the map, for example, C5. If C5 has an elephant on it, the player scores 5 points. If a player picks a square with a crocodile on it, he or she loses 3 points. After everyone has had five turns, add up the scores to find the winner. (Use a calculator if you get confused!) Then it is someone else's turn to put the features on the map.

95

PITCHING CAMP

After a day's travelling, explorers look for a place to camp. For a comfortable night's rest, they must choose the site carefully.

These are some of the things that real explorers look for.

Warm spot (not in a hollow or valley where cold air collects and causes frost)

Trees for a supply of wood

Nearby water supply

Dry, flat ground

 Shelter from the wind (Do not point the opening of a tent into the wind. Point it east, so it faces the sun in the morning.).

Shelters

Some explorers do not carry tents. Instead, they use natural materials such as sticks, leaves and rocks, and even snow, to build shelters.

Snow shelter. The hard, frozen walls stop the heat from bodies escaping.

Rock shelter - rocks piled up on the sides of a hollow with a roof made from sticks, grass and moss

Stick dome - like a teepee with long sticks in a circle, tied together at the top, then sticks and moss woven in between

Make your own shelter

Here are some easy
shelters to make, or
make up your own.

This is a good shelter indoors or out.

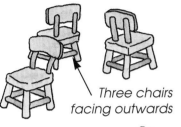

Three chairs
facing outwards

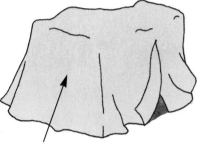

Large sheet or blanket draped over

In dry, warm weather, you might be
able to spend the night in your
shelter. Don't forget:

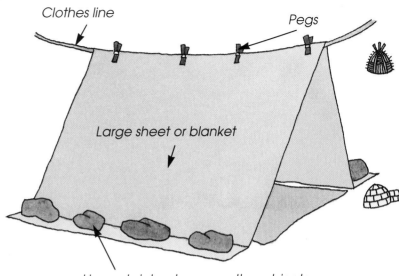

Clothes line

Pegs

Large sheet or blanket

Heavy bricks, stones or other objects

 Ask an adult to help you make this teepee.

Six very tall garden
canes tied around
with string at one
end. Spread the
other ends out in
a circle and push
them into the
ground.

Large
sheet or
blanket
wrapped
around

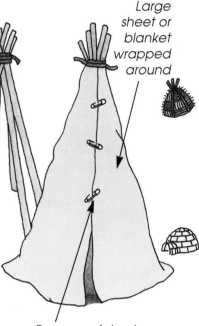

Pegs or safety pins
hold it together.

A flashlight

Comics
or a
book

Extra blankets

A radio or
walkman

Hot drink

Food rations

NORTH POLE TREK

In the Arctic it is always freezing cold and strong winds blow. Explorers have to travel across deep snow and ice on snowmobiles.

In this game, race the snowmobiles back to the igloos but watch out for the polar bears and the ice-holes!

You need:

Big sheet of white cardboard or posterboard (15$\frac{1}{4}$ in x 20$\frac{1}{2}$ in)
Thick and thin colored paper
Felt-tip pens, straws
Poster-tack, glue
Craft knife, scissors, ruler

Igloos

Draw and cut out four igloos from thick paper. Give each one a number which will be its score. Bend along the dotted lines and glue the bases to the cardboard.

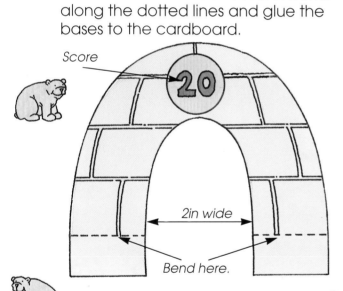

Score

20

2in wide

Bend here.

Polar bears

Draw and cut out five polar bears, with bases, from thick paper. Copy these or make up your own.

To make the bears stand up, bend along the dotted line.

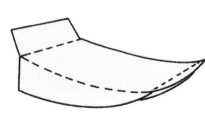

4in

1in

Snowmobiles

Copy this shape onto thin paper. Cut out three or four in different colors. Score and bend along the dotted lines to make them stand up.

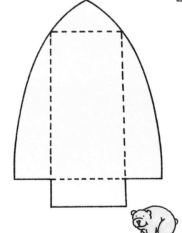 

Board

Measure and draw lines 2in in from each side. Score and bend up slightly.

Glue the igloos along one end of the board.

Use a craft knife to cut out several ice holes.

Stick the polar bears on with poster-tack.

How to play

Prop up the board on books so that it slopes down towards the end with the igloos.

Each player in turn takes three tries at blowing the snowmobiles into the igloos. Use a straw and blow at the turned-up tail of the snowmobile. Score points for each one you get into an igloo. The number of points will depend on which igloo you enter.

If you fall through an ice hole or crash into a hungry polar bear, you lose your turn.

At the end of the game, the players add up their scores. The winner is the person who has scored the most points.

JUNGLE SAFARI

Jungles, or tropical rainforests, are hot, steamy places overgrown with trees, vines and other plants. They grow so thickly that explorers must use knives to cut their way through.

Tropical rainforests grow close to the Equator, where it is very hot and damp. It rains nearly every day, often with thunder and lightning. After a downpour, it looks as if the jungle is steaming.

All kinds of amazing, colourful birds and animals live in the jungle. Here is an idea for a mural for your bedroom wall.

You need:

Roll of plain wallpaper or lining paper
Colored paper
Felt-tip pens, paints
Cellophane tape
Poster-tack or glue
Scissors

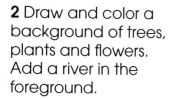

1 Tape strips of wallpaper along the wall. Ask an adult's permission first!

If you stick each creature on with poster-tack you can change around the scene whenever you like.

2 Draw and color a background of trees, plants and flowers. Add a river in the foreground.

3 Draw animals, birds, insects and fish on paper. Color them in and cut them out. Stick them onto the background.

Here are some shapes for you to copy. Look in books and magazines for pictures of other jungle creatures to copy.

Butterfly

Macaw

Monkey

Sloth

Tree frog

Alligator

Python

Piranha fish

Jaguar

Hummingbird

The jungle is divided into levels from the treetops to the ground. Different plants and animals live at each level.

NATURE TRAIL

Many real explorers travelled through unknown lands, hoping to find new kinds of plants or animals. If you make this nature trail kit you can be a wildlife explorer too.

Explore the local park, woods, countryside, or your garden. Don't go exploring on your own. Take a group of friends or an adult with you.

Keep a record of what you see in a special notebook. Divide each page into four columns headed Date, Time, Place and Description.

Date	Place	Time	Description
Mon 7th	Garden	3.30pm	Green caterpillar
Tue 8th	Apple tree	4.00pm	Blue b
Fri 10th	Front lawn	8.30 am	
Sat 11th	By the compost	10.00 am	Very hairy caterpillar
Sun 12th	Park	11.30 am	Big blue

Cover your notebook with colored paper and either draw or cut out and glue on paper bird, animals, plants and insects.

Bug jar

Here is a fun way to pick up tiny insects to examine without harming them. Release them as soon as you have studied them. Do not leave the jar in the sun or the insects will die.

Draw around one end of each tube onto the lid. Cut out the circles to make holes for the tubes. The tubes must fit tightly.

You need:

Small glass jar with plastic lid
11³/₄in length plastic tubing x ¹/₄in diameter
8in length plastic tubing x ¹/₄ in diameter
Craft knife
Pencil
Cotton balls
Gauze

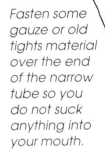

Don't suck up insects that are too big as they might get damaged in the tube.

Fasten some gauze or old tights material over the end of the narrow tube so you do not suck anything into your mouth.

Cotton wool for a soft landing

Elastic band

Gauze or piece of old tights

Place the thick tube over bug.

Suck in through the thin tube.

Keeping caterpillars

If you find a caterpillar, bring it home with some of the plant it was feeding on.

Keep it in a large jar or glass tank. It must be in a container big enough for its wings to spread when it turns into a butterfly or moth.

Watch it turn into a chrysalis and then, two or three weeks later, into a moth or butterfly.

Don't keep your moth a prisoner - let it go when it is strong enough to fly.

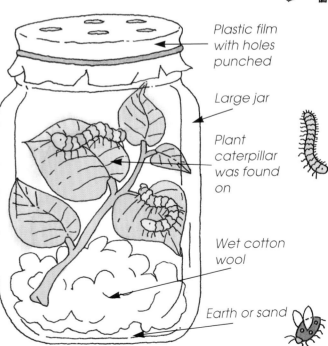

Plastic film with holes punched

Large jar

Plant caterpillar was found on

Wet cotton wool

Earth or sand

UNDERSEA ADVENTURE

Under the sea there is an amazing world to explore.
It is full of strange and colorful wildlife, dramatic
landscapes and exciting finds, such as sunken treasure.

Some undersea explorers dive with air tanks
called aqualungs attached to them. With
these they can explore the shallower ocean
waters. Deep-sea explorers travel down
thousands of meters in small submarines called
submersibles.

Diving experiment

Here is a diving experiment to try.

You need:

Empty plastic bottle (1.5 liter)
Plastic from a food carton
Pen top
Rubber band
Plasticine or poster-tack

*Make sure you draw th
diver narrow enough to
fit through the bottle ne*

1 Draw a diver onto the
plastic using a pencil.
Cut it out. Decorate
using waterproof paints.

*Don't use a pen top
with a hole here!*

2 Stick a small lump of
poster-tack or plasticine
around the pen top
without blocking the
open end.

*Don't cover the
opening.*

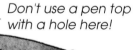

*A slim, pointed
pen top is best.*

3 Fix the pen top to the
diver with the rubber
band.

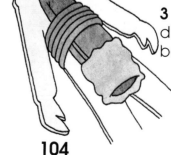

4 Fill the bottle almost full with water. Put in the diver - it should just float.

5 Screw on the bottle cap. Squeeze the bottle and the diver will sink to the bottom. Let go and he or she will rise to the top.

You could decorate the bottle by sticking paper shapes of fish, seaweed, coral, even a sunken ship, around the outside with glue or double-sided tape.

If the diver is too light, or sinks, empty the bottle, take the diver out and adjust the amount of Plasticine. You may have to do this a few times to get it right.

Wrap plastic film around to keep them in place.

Diving language

In the water, real divers "talk" to one another in sign language like this:

Going up

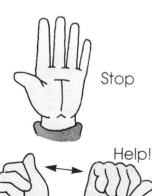

Stop

OK

Going down

Help!

Something wrong

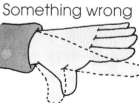

LOST TREASURE

Many explorers dream of being the first to discover a
long-lost ancient city, or finding treasure that has
stayed hidden for thousands of years.

Expeditions into unknown places can
be difficult and dangerous. These
explorers have found their way into a
hidden chamber inside a pyramid.
But the entrance is closing behind
them! Can you help them find
another way out?

SPACE JOURNEY

In space, there is no air to breathe and no gravity to stop astronauts floating away. Outside their space capsules, they must wear thick spacesuits for protection and carry oxygen tanks so that they can breathe.

A shellsuit or baggy tracksuit makes a great spacesuit.

Make a laser gun from an empty plastic bottle that has a handle. Decorate with foil and colored paper.

Oxygen pack

You need:

*Large piece of cardboard or posterboard
2 empty plastic bottles
Plastic tubing
Colored paper
String, cellophane tape*

Place one end of the plastic tubing through a hole in the side of the helmet.

Make holes at the top.

Thread through string, long enough to cross over at the front and tie behind your back

Place the other end of the plastic tubing in a bottle top and secure with tape.

Tape or glue the plastic bottles to the cardboard.

Paint or cover cardboard with aluminum foil or paper.

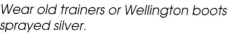

Wear old trainers or Wellington boots sprayed silver.

Helmet

You need:

Cardboard box big enough to fit over
  your head
Scissors or craft knife
Aluminum foil
Colored paper
Glue
String

1 Open out all the box flaps. Cut
away the shaded areas at the
front and back of the box.

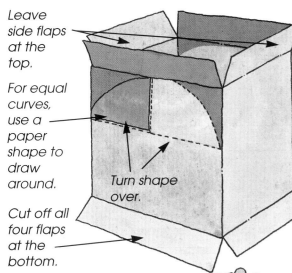

Leave
side flaps
at the
top.

For equal
curves,
use a
paper
shape to
draw
around.

Turn shape
over.

Cut off all
four flaps
at the
bottom.

2 Cut out a square at the front for
your face. Bend over side flaps and
glue to curves.

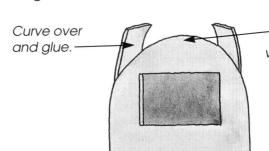

Curve over
and glue.

Cover
gap
with foil.

3 Cut out a curved shape at each
side so that the helmet fits over your
shoulders. Make holes back and
front, thread string through and tie
under arms.

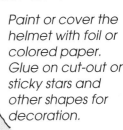

Paint or cover the
helmet with foil or
colored paper.
Glue on cut-out or
sticky stars and
other shapes for
decoration.

Alien masks

Space scientists say
there could be other
life in the universe.
What do you think the
"aliens" might look like?
Here are some alien
masks to make.
Attach string to the
sides to tie around
your head.

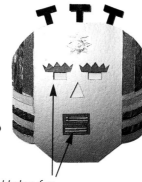

Holes for
eyes and
mouth.

Thin cardboard

Antennae
made from pipe
cleaners and
pieces of cork

Colored paper
shapes glued on

Famous explorers

 The **Vikings** from Scandinavia began exploring new territory as early as the 9th century, settling in Iceland and Greenland. It is now thought that Vikings in their longships were the first Europeans to discover America.

David Livingstone was the first European to walk right across Africa. He went missing in 1868 while searching for the source of the River Nile. Three years later he was found by Henry Stanley, an American who set out with an expedition to find him.

In the past, it was unusual for women to become explorers. **Mary Kingsley** began to travel in 1893. On her travels through Africa she faced many dangers and collected rare specimens of fish and insects.

 Jacques Cousteau is a famous modern underwater explorer. He designed and experimented with new diving equipment and was the first to use underwater photography to learn more about sea-life.

In 1492, **Christopher Columbus** set sail from Spain for the Far East. He wanted to prove that the world was round not flat, so he sailed west instead of east. After two months, land was sighted. Columbus thought he had reached China, but he had in fact arrived at the Bahamas, off the coast of America. He returned to Spain a hero, and died without ever knowing the importance of his discovery.

Meriwether Lewis and **William Clark** were the first Europeans to explore America from the Mississippi River to the west coast. It took them over two years, from 1804 to 1806, to travel 13,000 kilometers.

In 1911, a team of Norwegians, led by **Roald Amundsen**, became the first people to reach the South Pole. They just beat a British expedition led by **Captain Robert Scott**. Sadly, on the return journey, all five members of the British team died from the cold.

Mountain explorers, **Sir Edmund Hillary** and **Tenzing Norgay**, were the first men to reach the top of Mount Everest, the highest mountain in the world. They did this in 1952.

In 1961, Soviet cosmonaut **Yuri Gagarin** became the first person to travel into space. In 1969, US astronaut **Neil Armstrong** became the first person to walk on the moon.

Survival tips

In the desert

Carry as much water as possible. If you run out, conserve the water in your body by travelling at night when it is cooler. Some desert plants contain water that you can try to squeeze out.

In the tropics

Cover your body against mosquitoes and other insects. Shake out your shoes, clothes and bedding before use in case insects or snakes have crawled in!

In polar regions

Prevent frostbite by keeping warm, eating and drinking warm drinks.

In the water

Wear a lifejacket at all times. Keep your head out of water. Use air-filled clothes to help keep you afloat.

Signalling

The following are recognized as distress signals throughout the world.

Use stones and pieces of wood to write on the ground. Find a large clearing that can be spotted from the air.

Help!

Need medical equipment

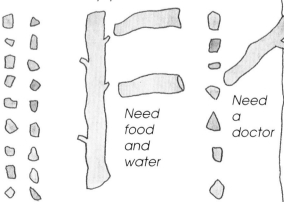

Need food and water

Need a doctor

Aliens Beings from another planet.

Antarctic The frozen land surrounding the South Pole.

Aqualung Diving apparatus with air carried in containers on the diver's back.

Arctic The frozen land and sea around the North Pole.

Climate The type of weather in an area.

Equator The imaginary line around the middle of the Earth.

Expedition An organized journey to explore a place.

Gravity The force that keeps us on the ground.

Igloo Dome-shaped shelter built from blocks of snow.

Kit Supplies and equipment.

Navigate Find the way, usually following a map.

North Pole The point on the Earth that is furthest north.

Pitch camp Set up a shelter for the night.

Pyramid An ancient Egyptian monument.

Rations Share of food and water.

Route Planned path of a journey.

Safari A journey, especially in Africa.

Shelter Place to keep you dry, warm and comfortable, such as a tent, cave, or shelter built from natural materials.

Site Place to pitch camp.

SOS Distress signal.

South Pole The point on the Earth that is furthest south.

Specimen Object collected for study.

Submersible Small submarine.

Supplies Food, water and equipment.

Survive To stay alive.

Terrain Ground or landscape.

Territory An area of land.

Trail A route or path.

Trek A long journey.

Tropical Climate that is hot and rainy.

DID YOU KNOW?

- The first explorers used the Moon, Sun and stars to find their way.

- The British explorer David Livingstone went missing in Africa for five years.

- Early explorers thought the world was flat and were afraid of falling off the edge.